Capital Without Borders

Capital Without Borders

Direct Investments and Strategic Insights for Economic Growth

Olga Kugatkina

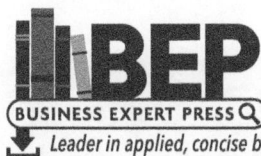

BEP

BUSINESS EXPERT PRESS

Leader in applied, concise business books

First published in 2025 by
Business Expert Press, LLC
222 East 46th Street, New York, NY 10017
www.businessexpertpress.com

ISBN-13: 978-1-63742-854-2 (paperback)
ISBN-13: 978-1-63742-855-9 (e-book)

Business Expert Press Economics and Public Policy Collection

First edition: 2025

10 9 8 7 6 5 4 3 2 1

EU SAFETY REPRESENTATIVE
Mare Nostrum Group B.V.
Mauritskade 21D
1091 GC Amsterdam
The Netherlands
gpsr@mare-nostrum.co.uk

Description

In today's global economy, mobilizing both domestic investment and foreign investment is crucial for sustaining economic growth and enhancing global competitiveness. Foreign direct investment (FDI) can be a powerful tool of national economic transformation. However, the flow of FDI is anything but predictable—it's dynamic, often concentrated in specific regions, creating both opportunities and hurdles for national economies. This uneven distribution can hinder technological advancement, particularly in countries with weak institutional frameworks, or, conversely, serve as a bridge to closing development gaps.

This book, *Capital without Borders: Direct Investments and Strategic Insights for Economic Growth*, explores how Foreign Direct Investment (FDI) serves as a transformative tool for economies seeking sustainable development and global integration. The subject is a comprehensive examination of FDI's role in driving innovation, growth, and competitiveness, focusing on investment strategies and allocation priorities that helped to realize FDI potential in full.

The book is designed for policy makers, business leaders, economists, academics, and all investment professionals involved in shaping economic policy, guiding corporate strategy, and establishing international economic collaboration, especially in the field of investments. Readers will benefit from an in-depth analysis of global investment trends, the motivations behind investment decisions, core factors impacting efficiency, and the impact of investments, and will see how the approaches to investment allocations and the significance and importance of the FDI role changed over time. Through a detailed analysis of lessons from transition economies such as Central Eastern Europe and China, as well as the current investment strategies of top donor nations, including the United States, Japan, China, and the European Union, the book offers practical recommendations for attracting the right kind of investments and optimizing investment strategies for maximum efficiency.

The findings and recommendations outlined in this book are designed to offer practical insights for policy makers, economists, and business leaders who seek to leverage FDI as a powerful catalyst for economic growth. By grounding these insights in a comprehensive analysis of international investment activity and macroeconomic regulation, the study presented in this book provides a robust framework for developing targeted FDI strategies.

The book will serve as a rigorous preparation for those who aspire to be an informed investor, equipping them with the tools and knowledge needed to navigate complex investment landscapes. Whether in the context of a specific country or broader global applications, the principles discussed here are particularly relevant for those involved in shaping economic policy and guiding national or corporate strategy. This book can also serve as an important source for academics, government officials, and private sector stakeholders, as it offers a summary of all key investment theories and models currently in use.

Contents

List of Figures and Tables

Figures

Tables

Introduction

In today's global economy, mobilizing both domestic and foreign investment is crucial for sustaining economic growth and enhancing global competitiveness. Foreign direct investment (FDI) can be a powerful tool for national economic transformation. However, the flow of FDI is anything but predictable—it's dynamic, often concentrated in specific regions, creating both opportunities and hurdles for national economies. This uneven distribution can hinder technological advancement, particularly in countries with weak institutional frameworks, or, conversely, serve as a bridge to closing development gaps. Maximizing FDI's potential requires more than simply welcoming foreign capital. This potential can only be realized if a country develops a strategy, establishes clear priorities for attracting foreign capital, implements effective regulatory mechanisms, and creates an equitable, investor-friendly environment.

Insights from International Investment Theories

This book begins by exploring the foundational role of FDI in economic transformation, analyzing its historical evolution and theoretical underpinnings through the lens of leading economists and scholars. The opening chapter delves into the development of FDI theories, tracing their relevance to contemporary global challenges. It examines the motivational drivers behind international investment decisions, including market-seeking, efficiency-seeking, and strategic asset-seeking behavior, and assesses theoretical and methodological approaches to analyzing FDI flows. By integrating the insights of renowned theorists such as J. Dunning, M. Porter, and T. Ozawa, R. Solow, J. Markusen, and others, the chapter offers a comprehensive perspective on how investment strategies have evolved to meet the demands of a rapidly shifting competitive environment. The book explores foundational frameworks that explain the direct and indirect effects of foreign direct investment and how national prosperity is built, revealing both the visible forces and the subtler dynamics that shift comparative advantage and shape long-term growth. The chapters also explore the tools and policies that enhance FDI's effectiveness, including macroeconomic regulations and mechanisms tailored to national priorities.

Strategic Sectoral Investment Priorities

Subsequent chapters build on this foundation, addressing how emerging economies have harnessed FDI to fuel growth and global integration. Drawing from the experiences of transition economies, the book evaluates strategies for channeling investments into sectors that drive innovation, technological advancement, and international competitiveness. Key lessons include the importance of aligning FDI flows with national goals, leveraging public-private partnerships (PPPs), and deploying fiscal and non-fiscal incentives to attract high-impact investments.

The book highlights the critical role of targeted investment policies in enhancing FDI's contribution to sustainable development. By analyzing the priorities of leading FDI donor countries and the macroeconomic tools they use to regulate capital flows, the book offers actionable insights for optimizing investment strategies. Mechanisms such as special investment zones, tax incentives, and infrastructure development are explored in detail, providing a roadmap for policymakers and business leaders.

Ukraine: Insights for Economic Transformation

In a dedicated chapter, the book examines Ukraine's potential to leverage FDI as a catalyst for economic growth. Using methodologies such as statistical analysis and scenario modeling, it assesses the correlation between FDI volumes and economic development, proposing practical mechanisms for identifying strategically important sectors and attracting investments to them. Drawing on best practices from transition economies and the pioneering work of international economists, the analysis underscores the importance of aligning FDI strategies with Ukraine's or any nation's unique economic context.

The findings reveal the critical role of institutional support, intergovernmental coordination, and strategic prioritization in creating a competitive investment environment. Furthermore, the book explores the development of sector-specific policies for industries such as aerospace, defense, technology, and agriculture, identifying their potential to drive economic modernization and global integration.

Ukraine's FDI-driven model can set a global precedent for post-conflict national growth. This strategy builds a compelling investment case by centering human development, prioritizing sustainable urban and infrastructure projects, and repurposing defense innovations for civilian applications. This multidimensional approach goes beyond restoring what was lost—it creates new pathways for technological advancement and economic diversification, embedding resilience in the national fabric.

Ukraine's reconstruction journey offers valuable lessons for the global economy. It highlights the importance of channeling FDI into sectors that drive long-term competitiveness, sustainability, and innovation. As global interest converges on Ukraine's renewal, its strategy can serve as a benchmark for how nations in crisis can use FDI to transform challenges into opportunities, ultimately achieving growth that is inclusive, innovative, and enduring.

Practical Significance of FDI and Its Broader Implications

The insights and recommendations presented in this book transcend theoretical discourse. Grounded in extensive research and real-world applications, the strategies outlined here have been instrumental in shaping legislative and strategic initiatives, including those of the Ukrainian Parliament and international organizations. The book serves as an essential resource for policy makers, corporate strategists, and academics seeking to harness FDI as a driver of sustainable growth.

By integrating advanced economic models, global best practices, and actionable frameworks, the book offers a robust foundation for shaping FDI strategies that align with national development goals. Its lessons extend beyond Ukraine, providing valuable guidance for other nations navigating the complexities of attracting and optimizing foreign investments in a rapidly evolving global landscape.

CHAPTER 1

Capital without Borders: How Direct Investments Transform Nations and Fuels Growth

1.1 Unpacking Foreign Direct Investment Theories and Process: What Drives Growth—Portfolio or Direct Investments?

The theoretical foundations of the investment process are not just an academic pursuit; they are vital to understanding and driving a nation's economic development. Activating the investment process significantly shapes a country's economic landscape, particularly in the organizational and legal frameworks that govern interactions between investment entities.

At its core, the investment process is a multifaceted economic category, requiring careful consideration of the relationships among participants, each driven by the twin goals of profit and social impact. To navigate this complex landscape effectively, investors and policy makers must possess both theoretical insight and practical experience. Understanding the systemic nature of the investment process reveals its profound impact on national economies and their trajectory of growth. Mastering this system is crucial for those who aim not just to navigate but also to shape the future of economic development.

First Principles: The investment process is inherently **systemic**, comprising **four essential elements**: the subject (the investor), the object (the investment), the relationship that binds them (the pursuit of returns), and the environment in which they operate (the investment environment).

This intricate relationship serves as the core, uniting all components into a cohesive and strategic framework.

A contemporary approach to the investment process redefines it as the strategic alignment of investors with targeted investment objects within specific environments, all with the goal of achieving calculated returns. At the center of this system lies the investment environment itself—a complex network of activities and conditions that ultimately shape the character and dynamics of investments.

Recognizing the distinctive attributes of this process is critical to designing effective strategies. **Key attributes that shape the process include**:

- **Scale and Long-Term Commitment:** Direct investments typically require significant capital and a long-term perspective, necessitating strategic planning and sustained commitment.
- **Subjective Decision Making:** Personal biases and varying perspectives influence investment decisions, highlighting the need to account for these subjective factors in strategy.
- **Environmental Interconnections:** Investments are intricately shaped by their surrounding environment, with external factors such as political stability and market conditions playing an important role in determining outcomes.
- **Macroeconomic Impact:** The dynamics and nature of the investment process influence key macroeconomic indicators such as gross domestic product (GDP), national growth, and living standards.

To fully understand the essence of the investment process, it must be connected to **key economic concepts: investment activity, investment attractiveness, investor behavior**, the **investment climate**, and the **broader investment environment**. The term "investment" has evolved since it entered the economic lexicon in the late 1970s and early 1980s. In macroeconomic theory, it refers to the **long-term allocation of public or private capital across various sectors**, both domestically and internationally, with the goal of generating returns. Simply put, **investment is the infusion of capital—whether from private or state sources—into the production of specific goods**.

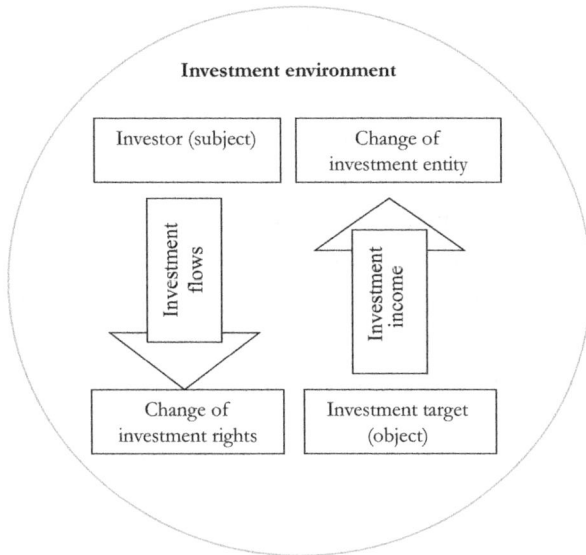

Figure 1.1 The investment process as a system

Yet, defining "investment" is not without its challenges. The term spans both broad and narrow interpretations, with various branches of economic science and practice assigning different meanings based on their scope, context, and objectives. In academic literature, investments are often framed as property rights or other assets subject to ownership. In its broadest sense, investment represents the commitment of capital with the goal of generating future returns. This infusion of capital should yield gains sufficient to compensate for the investor's risks and the opportunity cost associated with deferring immediate consumption.[1]

At its core, an investment represents the commitment of capital in the present, driven by the expectation of future returns. This forward-looking perspective is central to the nature of investments, defining them as present economic outlays with the aim of generating future gains. Ultimately, it is this inherent expectation of growth and return that shapes investment decisions.

Strategic View: From a macroeconomic perspective, investment plays a central role in driving economic growth through capital accumulation and the deepening of the capital stock, a process often measured in practice by gross fixed capital formation. Expanding an economy's productive capacity depends on multiple factors: timely upgrading of fixed assets, advances in science and technology, balanced development across strategic sectors, and the global competitiveness of domestically produced goods and services. Equally important are secure access to critical raw materials, resilient supply chains, and a stable policy environment that supports both economic dynamism and social cohesion. Together, all these elements contribute to a nation's economic trajectory.

Granular View: On the micro level, investments are vital for achieving a wide range of business objectives. They enable companies to expand operations, enhance product quality, reduce costs, modernize production, and maintain competitiveness in an ever-evolving marketplace.

Integrated Insights: Taken together, these perspectives underscore the indispensable role of investment in shaping outcomes at both the macroeconomic and enterprise levels. Beyond capital accumulation, investment enhances an economy's adaptability, enabling innovation, productivity growth, and entrepreneurial dynamism. It strengthens the capacity of both governments and firms to respond to shifting market conditions, technological disruption, and evolving national priorities. Strategic investment in infrastructure, education, and public services—all components of gross fixed capital formation—not only boosts economic output but also promotes social cohesion. Few forces shape a nation's long-term prosperity more decisively than investment, fueling everything from productivity gains and industrial competitiveness to the infrastructure that anchors modern life. By supporting global competitiveness and reinforcing economic resilience, investment acts as a stabilizing force essential for sustainable growth.

Strategic investments become indispensable in a domestic economy recovering from a crisis or transitioning to a growth phase. Businesses and organizations require substantial capital to restore stability, upgrade production capabilities, and improve product and service quality. However, domestic investment sources may fall short of supporting the necessary growth trajectory, creating an opening for foreign investors to contribute to the domestic economy.

Defining Investment: Unpacking the Diverse Perspectives Shaping Its Meaning

There is no single, universally accepted definition of foreign investment. Rather, it is interpreted through a spectrum of perspectives found in legal and economic literature and the legislative frameworks of various states. This multifaceted nature reflects the dynamic interplay of norms, perspectives, practices, and nuances that shape its meaning in today's global economy.

Foreign Direct Investment (FDI) is typically defined as an ownership stake substantial enough to grant the investor meaningful influence over the enterprise's management, signaling a long-term commitment to its growth and success. The most widely recognized definition comes from the International Monetary Fund (IMF) and the Organization for Economic Co-operation and Development (OECD): "Foreign Direct Investment typically involves a long-term relationship that reflects a lasting interest and significant influence by a resident entity in one economy (the direct investor) in an enterprise resident in another economy (the direct investment enterprise)".

The 10 percent ownership threshold is broadly accepted across international organizations, including the IMF, OECD, and World Trade Organization (WTO). This standard highlights not full control but rather a lasting interest and significant influence over the enterprise's operations.

A broader perspective defines foreign investment as capital deployed by a foreign entity to stimulate economic activity—whether or not local capital is involved—resulting in the creation of production facilities that contribute to the host country's economic growth and potential. Legal definitions expand on this, framing foreign investment as the flow of capital—regardless of type or form—transferred from one nation and invested in enterprises within another. These varied perspectives illustrate the complexities and nuances of the foreign investment process. It is more than a financial transaction; it represents a multidimensional process with structural implications—driven by the strategic interplay of economic influence and operational control.

FDI is distinguished from other forms by its long-term commitment. FDI typically involves a foreign entity establishing lasting influence or control over a business enterprise in another country. This influence can be achieved through equity ownership, management authority, or significant decision-making power. Unlike portfolio investments, which are driven by financial returns alone, FDI entails operational involvement, giving investors a stake in the management and strategic direction of the enterprise.

Finally, FDI must be understood through the lens of investor intent, focusing on the motives behind investment decisions. In this context, FDI refers to the transfer of assets—whether tangible or intangible—by a foreign company into another country, aimed at enhancing the investor's financial, technological, market, and competitive performance. It is not just about moving capital; it is about positioning the investor for growth and long-term success in the global marketplace.

From the definitions we have explored, we can now identify the **essential characteristics of FDI**:

- First, FDI involves the transfer of property, financial assets, or non-current assets by an investor to a foreign country, intended for use in business activities within the host country.
- Second, FDI is characterized by its long-term nature and substantial capital, sufficient to influence the management and strategic decisions of the target company.
- Third, FDI represents capital originating from abroad that is directly invested in enterprises in other countries.

According to the OECD, the IMF and the World Bank, FDI takes several primary forms, each reflecting different strategic intents and investment dynamics:

1. **Equity Investments**: The most common form of FDI, this involves an investor acquiring at least 10 percent of the voting power in a foreign business. Equity investments are expected to provide influence over management and establish a lasting interest of investors in the management of the enterprise.

2. **Mergers and Acquisitions**: Through this form, investors acquire a controlling share or completely take over an existing enterprise abroad. This approach is often pursued to establish a presence in foreign markets, integrate into global value chains (GVCs), and gain access to new technologies and resources.

3. **Greenfield Investments**: In contrast to mergers and acquisitions, greenfield investments involve the establishment of new operations abroad from the ground up. These investments have a significant impact, as they contribute directly to the host economy by creating new jobs, building production facilities, diversifying economic activity, and boosting overall economic growth.

4. **Joint Ventures and Strategic Alliances**: These forms of FDI involve cooperation with foreign companies to create a new, jointly owned enterprise. This form of FDI allows for risk-sharing and combining strengths in foreign markets where local knowledge and the presence of a local partner support market entry and long-term growth.

5. **Vertical and Horizontal Investments**: Vertical FDI occurs when a company invests in foreign operations that are part of its supply chain, either upstream (suppliers) or downstream (distributors). Horizontal FDI happens when a firm replicates its home country–based activities at the same value chain stage in a host country.

Each of these FDI forms not only transfers capital but also facilitates the movement of expertise, technology, and industry practices across borders, reinforcing the interconnectedness of global economies.

FDI can be categorized into two primary types: transcontinental investment and transnational investment. Transcontinental investments are typically motivated by market access, allowing companies to position themselves closer to their target markets. **Transnational investments**, on the other hand, focus on minimizing costs by locating operations in neighboring or lower-cost countries. Both strategies play a vital role in global economic integration.[2]

What Matters More: Portfolio or Direct Investments?

The impact of foreign capital on a nation's economy is defined by the nuanced dynamics between direct and portfolio investments. FDI holds a special impact, offering investors the opportunity to not only invest in businesses but also exert control over their operations. In contrast, portfolio investments enter a country primarily through the purchase of securities facilitated by international financial institutions, investment funds, export credit agencies, and banks.

While there are instances where portfolio investments may resemble the effects of direct investments—such as when acquisitions lead to expanded production capacity or drive technological innovation—these remain exceptions. Typically, host countries view portfolio investments with caution, as they are often associated with speculative activities that contribute little to the real economy.

Portfolio investments typically limit investor rights to receiving dividends. However, exceptions do exist. International corporations can exert influence through portfolio investments, particularly when there is a significant dispersion of shares among investors or when additional contractual obligations, such as licensing agreements or service contracts, limit a company's independence. This ability to wield control without full ownership has made portfolio investments an increasingly attractive vehicle for investors.

The predominant method for portfolio investments is the purchase of shares on the global stock market. In the late twentieth century, the United States dominated nearly half of the global stock market, with Japan accounting for 13 percent. The combined share of the seven leading developed nations—the United States, United Kingdom, Germany, Japan, France, Italy, and Canada—accounts for approximately 80 percent of global stock market value. This figure is significantly higher than their combined share of global GDP, underscoring the outsized prominence of their stock markets relative to their economic size. This disparity illustrates how the world's leading financial markets exert a global influence that far exceeds their economic weight—shaping investment flows, policy priorities, and the contours of global powers.

The evolution of the stock market has been shaped by key economic factors: the shift to floating exchange rates, deregulation of financial markets, increased liquidity, and a surge in institutional investors. These changes fueled the rise of international capital flows and led to significant advancements in portfolio diversification strategies.

Since the 2000s, portfolio investments have grown due to the internationalization of stock exchanges, the removal of restrictions on foreign companies accessing these markets, and the increasing participation of pension funds and credit institutions. Stock exchanges themselves have undergone radical transformations, expanding into new markets and gaining global influence. By the late 1990s, the exponential growth in stock trading volumes prompted exchanges to adopt electronic trading, establishing infrastructure for round-the-clock global transactions.

The changes in the global economy and the rise of portfolio investments have coincided with advancements in technology, globalization, and the centralization of financial power. Stock markets have become more integrated, with innovations in securitization and computerized trading systems reshaping the financial landscape. However, **while portfolio investment continues to dominate capital flows, FDI remains an important source of capital for developing and transitioning economies.**

FDI is crucial for countries seeking access to modern production technologies, management expertise, and marketing strategies. The main avenues for attracting FDI include joint ventures, establishing foreign-owned enterprises, production-sharing agreements, and the creation of free economic zones. FDI often takes the form of acquiring shares in local companies, reinvesting profits, or providing long-term loans.

The long-term nature of FDI makes it challenging for investors to quickly exit, thereby increasing risk exposure. However, this same long-term characteristic also positions FDI as a strategic tool for countries aiming to stimulate economic growth, making it an essential form of foreign capital, particularly for developing nations. Even amid volatility, FDI distinguishes itself through the depth and durability of its contributions. It's not just about capital—it's about technology diffusion and growth, transferring management expertise and critical market insights. It is these elements that make FDI crucial for long-term economic growth, particularly in developing nations. While short-term disruptions may slow its pace, the strategic benefits of FDI ensure that it remains a vital engine of global economic integration.

1.2 The Evolution of Investment Theories: Shaping Modern Investment Strategies

The evolution of investment theories mirrors the shifting balance between economic thought, government interventions, and market dynamics. In today's increasingly complex global economy—interconnected yet fragmented—understanding these theoretical shifts is critical for policymakers, investors, and business leaders seeking to anticipate disruption and shape long-term competitive strategy.

A Brief History

Investment theory traces its roots to the mercantilist era of the sixteenth and seventeenth centuries, when mercantilists emphasized maintaining a sufficient volume of capital in circulation within a nation to stimulate investment and lower the cost of capital. This perspective prevailed until the late nineteenth century, when the marginalist school emerged, bringing forth concepts of marginal utility and market equilibrium. These principles allowed for a more precise analysis of international capital flows, directly linking them to the factors influencing equilibrium in global markets.

From the early mercantilists to the marginalist economists of the late nineteenth century, investment theory evolved within the framework of market rationality and self-regulating mechanisms. It was the Great Depression, a global economic collapse of unprecedented scale, that exposed the fragility of those assumptions. In response, John Maynard Keynes offered a radically new framework: investment decisions are not mechanical responses to interest rates, they are influenced by uncertainty, expectations, and collective behaviors. He emphasized the role of government in stabilizing investment and demand.

John Maynard Keynes introduced the concept of the "**marginal efficiency of capital**," emphasizing that investment is only justified when its expected return exceeds the interest rate on loans. He further advanced investment theory by highlighting the crucial role of government intervention in stabilizing the economy during periods of recession or depression. Rejecting the idea that the investment process would automatically regulate itself, Keynes recognized the limitations of relying solely on interest rates to manage capital markets. He argued that during economic downturns, private sector decisions to cut back on investment and consumption would exacerbate the downturn. To counter this, Keynes advocated for active government intervention, including lowering interest rates and increasing public spending to stimulate demand. For Keynes, generating aggregate demand—including investment resources—was essential to economic recovery and growth.[3]

The foreign direct investment landscape as we know it today began to take shape in the 1960s, a decade that marked the expansion of multinational corporations (MNCs) and the growing need for global production capabilities. Firms from capital-abundant nations sought to extend their reach beyond their home markets, driven by innovations in production and increasing demand from global consumers. As cross-border ambitions intensified and logistics and communication channels improved, multinational enterprises (MNEs) became prominent players in the global economy, leveraging ownership advantages to establish operations abroad. This foundational stage, which witnessed the gradual liberalization of capital controls and the dismantling of trade barriers, laid the groundwork for the modern FDI process. By the 1970s, the flow of FDI had risen substantially, with firms increasingly viewing foreign investment as a key component of their global expansion strategy.

Since the 1960s, significant theoretical advancements have shaped the field of FDI. Foundational frameworks such as **Vernon's Product Lifecycle Theory, Dunning's Eclectic Paradigm, Porter's Competitive Advantage Theory, Hymer's Market Power Theory, Transaction Cost Theory**, and **Technological Accumulation Theory** have emerged to explain the motivations and strategies behind FDI. These theories **highlight the competitive advantages that firms and countries derive from factors such as innovation, market imperfections, and transaction costs**. Their insights have profoundly influenced economic policies and industrial strategies aimed at enhancing national competitiveness and guiding international investment activities.

Each theory offers a distinct perspective on why firms invest abroad, focusing on market structure, firm-specific advantages, and the constantly evolving global economic landscape. As such, these frameworks have become indispensable tools for policy makers and business leaders navigating the complexities of international investment.

Among these contributions, **Kiyoshi Kojima and Terutomo Ozawa's "Macroeconomic Model of Direct Investment"** is especially important in the context of Japanese investments. Kojima's theory distinguishes between trade-oriented FDI, which benefits both the investing and host countries and anti-trade-oriented FDI, which can disrupt local economies. Historically, Japanese investments have been trade-oriented—boosting exports from the host country—whereas American FDI has often focused on market control, sometimes leading to anti-trade effects. Kojima's model highlights the positive impact of trade-oriented FDI in strengthening the comparative advantages of both countries involved. However, its applicability is limited when examining capital flows between developed economies with similar economic structures and production factors.[4]

R. Aliber's Currency Premium Theory, introduced in the 1970s, emphasizes the role of exchange rates in FDI decisions. According to the theory, firms from countries with strong currencies are more likely to invest abroad, particularly in countries with weaker currencies, as they can borrow more cheaply. This exchange-rate disparity creates a "currency premium," providing investors from strong-currency countries with an advantage in financing capital expenditures in weaker-currency regions. Aliber's theory highlights the significance of currency differences in driving cross-border investment but faces limitations, especially when explaining cross-investments between regions with minimal exchange-rate disparities or reverse flows, where firms from weak-currency countries invest in stronger-currency regions.[5]

R. Mundell's theory of FDI, grounded in the impact of restrictive trade policies such as high tariffs, posits that firms from capital-abundant countries invest in capital-scarce nations to bypass trade barriers. However, like Aliber's theory, Mundell's model faces challenges in distinguishing between direct and portfolio investments, limiting its ability to fully address the control and ownership issues that are central to FDI.[6]

John Dunning's **Eclectic Paradigm (OLI Framework)**, first introduced in 1976 and further developed in his book *Explaining International Production* (1988), remains one of the most comprehensive frameworks for analyzing FDI decisions. Dunning's framework integrates three key factors—Ownership, Location, and Internalization Advantages—to explain why companies engage in FDI and how they select locations and modes of international production.

- **Ownership Advantage (O)**: Refers to the unique assets or capabilities that give a firm a competitive edge over local firms in foreign markets. These may include proprietary technology, brand strength, managerial expertise, or economies of scale.
- **Location Advantage (L)**: Relates to the specific characteristics of the host country that make it attractive for FDI, such as access to natural resources, favorable market conditions, low labor costs, infrastructure, and a stable political environment.
- **Internalization Advantage (I)**: Refers to the benefits a firm gains by controlling operations in foreign markets rather than licensing, franchising, or outsourcing. This control allows firms to protect proprietary knowledge, reduce transaction costs, and maintain supply chain control.

Dunning's eclectic paradigm is pivotal in understanding how countries evolve as either net exporters or net recipients of FDI. It offers valuable insights into how a country can transition from being a net recipient of FDI to becoming a significant outward investor.[7]

Dunning's **Investment Development Path (IDP)**, developed with Rajneesh Narula in 1996, builds on the Eclectic Paradigm by examining the relationship between a country's economic development and its FDI activity.[8] The IDP suggests that countries initially start as net recipients of FDI (negative Net Outward Investment, or NOI), but as they develop, they begin to invest abroad, eventually becoming net exporters of FDI (positive NOI). The model outlines five stages of this progression, with each stage reflecting shifts in a country's economic development, competitive advantages, and integration into the global economy:

1. **Low-Income Economies**: Characterized by limited FDI inflows due to low levels of industrialization and economic development, often reliant on agriculture.

2. **Transitioning Economies**: As industrialization progresses, these economies begin to attract FDI, focusing on manufacturing and infrastructure development.

3. **Emerging Economies**: Significant economic growth drives FDI inflows, with countries developing capabilities in R&D and diversifying their industries.

4. **Developed Economies**: Advanced technological capabilities and strong outward FDI characterize this stage, with firms investing abroad to leverage competitive advantages.

5. **High-Income Economies with High Outward FDI**: At this stage, economies are fully integrated into global markets and often serve as major sources of FDI for emerging and developing nations.

The IDP provides a dynamic framework for understanding how economic development shapes FDI patterns over time, offering valuable insights into the evolving nature of global investment flows.

From **2000 to 2024**, several key economic concepts have evolved in relation to FDI, reflecting shifts in global dynamics, technological advancements, and geopolitical changes.

Global Value Chains (GVCs) and FDI: Research from Columbia University expanded the GVC concept, highlighting how FDI integrates with global production networks. Initially, the fragmentation of production encouraged FDI flows to developing countries offering cost advantages in specific segments of GVCs. However, geopolitical tensions and the pandemic led companies to reassess investment locations, seeking more resilient supply chains.[9]

Economic Complexity and FDI: Research from Harvard's Growth Lab (Hausmann et al.) and Harvard Business School (Alfaro) highlights the role of economic complexity in attracting FDI. Countries with more diverse and sophisticated economies are better positioned to benefit from FDI, as these investments often generate significant spillover effects in technology transfer, productivity, and long-term economic growth. These countries typically possess better infrastructure, higher-quality human capital, and greater institutional capacity—all of which enhance their ability to attract and benefit from FDI.[10]

Geoeconomic Fragmentation: Recent research—including contributions from Stanford, the IMF, and the Hoover Institution—has analyzed how rising geopolitical tensions and regional conflicts are reshaping global FDI patterns. Investors increasingly favor politically stable regions aligned with their home countries, a trend known as "friend-shoring." This strategy reflects a broader shift in which companies and governments aim to reduce exposure to global instability by investing in geopolitically aligned regions.[11]

The evolution of investment theories reflects the dynamic, complex nature of the global economy. As the focus shifts toward knowledge-based investments and human capital, the drivers of competitive advantage continue to evolve. **Understanding these theories is crucial for policy makers, investors, and business leaders navigating the complexities of international investments.** Fluctuations in FDI demonstrate that sustained global competitiveness depends on adaptability of investment strategies as well as on the ability to foresight structural changes and design forward-looking, adaptive strategies.

The Evolution of the Modern FDI Landscape: Defining Trends from 1960 to Today

This foundational period, marked by the gradual liberalization of capital controls and opening of markets to trade, laid the groundwork for the FDI we recognize today. By the 1970s, FDI flows surged as corporations integrated foreign investments into their global strategies, marking the dawn of modern FDI. This analysis explores the critical stages of FDI's evolution, highlighting its key transformations across the decades.

The Formation of Modern FDI (1960s–1970s): The 1960s and 1970s marked the genesis of contemporary FDI, driven by the rise of multinational corporations (MNCs) whose domestic production capacities could no longer meet the demands of expanding export markets. In response, these corporations began establishing production facilities abroad, giving rise to FDI as we know it today. During this phase, the primary focus of FDI was international expansion. Neighboring countries with large domestic markets became prime investment destinations, setting a pattern for the decades ahead. Despite this rise in international expansion, FDIs during these decades were constrained by stringent government regulations and controlled capital flows, limiting foreign companies' access to certain markets.

Regionalization of Investment (1980s): By the 1980s, foreign investment entered a transformative phase, driven by the growth and consolidation of transnational corporations. No longer focused solely on individual neighboring markets, MNCs expanded to entire macro regions, establishing foreign production facilities to cater to regional demands. Industrial sectors such as manufacturing, automobiles, and consumer goods were prominent in cross-border investments during this period. The FDI of this period was driven by MNCs' strategic intent to optimize production costs, expand market access, and achieve economies of scale. The focus on labor efficiency, tax optimization, and infrastructure connectivity reshaped regional dynamics, creating interlinked production hubs that defined the era.

Global Expansion and Liberalization (1990s): The 1990s ushered in the liberalization of international investments, opening the door for FDI expansion on a global scale. This decade is widely regarded as the period of fastest growth for MNCs, driven by global economic and political changes. Transnational corporations, having expanded beyond national and regional markets, pursued worldwide direct investments across sectors such as manufacturing, services, and research and development (R&D). The collapse of the Soviet Union, and the opening of Eastern Europe to foreign capital, marked a pivotal moment, as newly available markets drew in global corporations eager to expand their footprint and influence. For developing economies, the 1990s marked a turning point—liberalized regulatory frameworks and the privatization of previously state-owned enterprises attracted unprecedented FDI, driving rapid economic transformation across Central and Eastern Europe, China, India, and other parts of Asia and Latin America.

Strategic Shifts Post-2000: In the twenty-first century, the FDI landscape experiences another shift—investment decisions decoupled from local market capacity, to become increasingly driven by factors beyond market size, such as access to resources, tax advantages, and specialized labor pools. For example, German automotive companies shifted production to Eastern Europe, leveraging favorable tax regimes and lower labor costs.

The rise of knowledge-based industries and innovation-driven sectors marked a critical departure from traditional investment patterns. The investment focus started to shift away from traditional industries toward more dynamic, innovation-driven, and knowledge-based sectors. A nation's competitive edge is no longer defined by cheap labor or natural resources but defined, instead, by the quality of its human capital, education systems, and the integration of science and technology into production processes.

Globalization, the rise of emerging markets, and the growing dominance of multinational corporations—driven by continued trade liberalization and advances in technology—defined the decade of global expansion and integration that began in 2000. Strategic acquisitions, greenfield investments, and regional supply chain optimization allowed MNCs to seize opportunities in rapidly growing economies such as China, India, and Brazil. Developed nations—especially in North America, Europe and Japan—remained major sources of outbound FDI, reinforcing their global economic influence. Meanwhile, developing nations are experiencing a gradual erosion of regulatory power as global corporations exert increasing pressure, reducing the ability of states to manage foreign capital inflows effectively.

Crisis and Resilience (2008–2020): The 2008 financial crisis exposed the vulnerabilities of economies heavily reliant on FDI, leading to a **temporary retreat of capital to safer markets**. This prompted a revaluation of investment strategies, with corporations prioritizing resilience over rapid expansion. FDI sharply declined from its peak in 2007, at US$2 trillion, to US$1.2 trillion in 2009. Gradual post-crisis recovery saw a **renewed focus on regionalization** and a **continuous pivot toward sustainable and technology-focused investments**, with China emerging as a dominant force in both outbound and inbound FDI. By 2015, global FDI had recovered to nearly US$2 trillion, with much of it flowing into knowledge-based industries and digital economies.

Geopolitical Fragmentation and Strategic Autonomy (2020–Present): The COVID-19 pandemic and rising geopolitical tensions have fundamentally reshaped FDI. As nations reassess global supply chains, investment strategies have shifted toward localization and "friend-shoring," prioritizing partnerships with aligned economies. Critical industries, such as semiconductors and pharmaceuticals, now dominate FDI agendas, reflecting a growing emphasis on national security and strategic resilience. This era marks a departure from global integration toward a more fragmented yet intentional approach to foreign investments.

From its origins as a mechanism for economic expansion to its current role in fostering resilience and innovation, FDI has continually adapted to the evolving demands of the global economy. As nations and corporations navigate the uncertainties of geopolitical fragmentation and technological transformation, FDI remains a cornerstone of economic strategy. Its ability to fuel growth, drive technological advancements, and enable strategic autonomy cements its status as an essential tool for shaping the economic future.

1.3 What Drives Foreign Direct Investment? Uncovering Key Motives for Corporations, Recipient Nations, and Donor Nations

Foreign Direct Investment (FDI) is far more than a mere financial transaction—it represents a nuanced decision-making process driven by multiple layers of strategic intent. As global economic landscapes grow increasingly intricate, FDI motives have evolved, blending financial objectives with technological advancements, geopolitical strategy, and competitive positioning. These complex motivations shape cross-border investments, making it crucial for policymakers, investors, and economists alike to deeply understand the forces driving FDI. Ultimately, the motivations behind FDI are deeply embedded in broader macroeconomic dynamics—from capital flows and balance of payments to industrial policy and technological diffusion.

1.3.1 What Drives Multinational Corporations (MNCs) to See Foreign Markets as the Key to Sustained Success?

FDI theories and analyses of global capital flows reveal four distinct categories of motives, each reflecting the strategic priorities that drive MNCs to invest abroad.

1. **Financial and Economic Motives**

    At its core, FDI is about the pursuit of higher returns on capital. Whether through tapping into surplus capital or gaining access to cheaper resources and strategic tax regimes or taking advantage of favorable tax regimes, companies are constantly seeking ways to generate additional profit and reduce costs. **MNCs from capital-abundant countries are particularly driven by the opportunity to deploy surplus capital in regions with lower operational costs, where labor and resources are less expensive.**

    The need to achieve cost efficiencies while maintaining competitiveness determines many FDI activities today. **Economic incentives such as tax breaks and deregulation play a significant role in attracting**

Table 1.1 Key motives

1. Financial and economic objectives	• Achieving higher returns on capital • Generating additional profit from surplus capital • Reducing costs through access to cheaper resources and strategic tax regimes
2. Technological advancement and innovation	• Accessing advanced high-tech industries (e.g., artificial intelligence, biotechnology) • Investing in R&D infrastructure (technology parks, digital innovation hubs) • Leveraging scientific and human capital
3. Market expansion and competitive positioning	• Expanding global presence • Capturing new and emerging markets • Securing a dominant position in key industries and gaining competitive advantages through strategic alignments
4. Geopolitical and strategic alignment	• Aligning investments with politically stable and strategically important regions • Mitigating risks through "friend-shoring" in geopolitically aligned countries • Ensuring supply chain resilience and national security

MNCs, particularly in emerging markets where the economic environment is favorable for capital investments.

2. Technological and Innovation Motives

Amid accelerating technological transformation, FDI has increasingly pivoted toward technology and innovation-driven motives. As MNCs navigate the digital age, access to cutting-edge industries such as artificial intelligence (AI), biotechnology, and advanced manufacturing has become one of the key factors shaping investment decisions. **Strategic asset-seeking FDI contributes to technology spillovers and innovation, strengthening productivity and long-term competitiveness at the macro level.** This shift reflects a broader strategic necessity with a dual intent on the part of MNCs: to adopt new technologies and to position themselves as leaders in shaping the future of these sectors.

MNCs are now focusing on investments in research and development (R&D), technology hubs, and innovation ecosystems to stay ahead of the curve. By establishing a presence in markets known for their technological prowess—such as Silicon Valley for tech startups or Shenzhen for hardware innovation—these firms leverage the expertise of local scientific communities and local human capital to maintain their competitive edge. This allows companies to access innovations and actively influence the trajectory of industry advancements.

As the digital economy evolves, the convergence of technological innovation, capital flows, and geopolitical dynamics is reshaping global investment strategies—*intensifying their influence on where, how, and why MNCs invest.* Nobel laureate **Paul Romer**, in his **Endogenous Growth Theory**, underscores the vital role of ideas and technological knowledge in driving long-term economic growth.[12] Endogenous Growth Theory **highlights the non-rival nature of knowledge**—meaning that the use of an idea by one firm does not diminish its availability to others. In this context, **FDI can be positioned as a critical channel in spreading technology, transferring knowledge, and disseminating innovations across borders, with MNCs acting as agents of innovation**.

Similarly, **Yuval Noah Harari**, a historian and intellectual with global influence and significance, suggests that control over data and digital infrastructure will soon rival the importance of traditional resources. Harari contends that the technological motives behind FDI are reshaping patterns of corporate growth and the geopolitical balance of power.[13] Investments in AI, biotechnology, and digital infrastructure will determine the future of industries and the global economy. The growing focus on technology and innovation reveals that **FDI motives have evolved beyond mere financial gain. It is about wielding influence over the technologies that will shape the future of industries, economies, and societies**.

3. Market Expansion and Competitive Positioning

What drives multinational corporations (MNCs) to venture beyond their home markets into unfamiliar—and often riskier—environments? The answer lies in the transformative power of FDI, a strategy that not only expands a company's global footprint but also reshapes its long-term competitive position. More than a tool for gaining new markets, FDI is a calculated move to secure sustained advantage.

By entering new markets, multinational corporations (MNCs) diversify revenue streams, extend their product offerings, and achieve economies of scale that enhance operational efficiency. This deliberate market expansion strengthen corporations' capacity to preempt competitors and assert strategic control in key sectors, consolidating their influence across the global economy. Consider the advantage of establishing a presence before rivals even recognize the opportunity.

What makes FDI particularly compelling is how MNCs align it with the lifecycle of their products—progressing through innovation, growth, maturity, and renewal. As innovations mature and growth stabilizes, savvy firms redeploy resources to new markets where demand remains high. By strategically aligning FDI with the product lifecycle, companies exploit geographic location–specific advantages, ensuring their offerings remain relevant and competitive for an extended term while leveraging unique product capabilities to capture larger market shares. Consider how firms introduce innovative or next-generation products in developed markets and later adapt these offerings to meet the evolving needs of emerging economies, maximizing their lifecycle value. FDI enables firms not only to respond to demand—but to influence and shape it over time. Companies that act early can establish a first-mover advantage in emerging markets, creating critical footholds that deter competitors and generate long-term value. These investments do more than enable expansion—they allow firms to internalize control over key assets (rather than rely on trade or licensing), outmaneuver competitors, and capture greater value in global markets.

4. Geopolitical and Strategic Alignment

Amid rising global tensions and market volatility, the dynamics of Foreign Direct Investment (FDI) are increasingly shaped by the geopolitical climate. Corporations are now focusing their investments on regions considered politically stable and strategically aligned, in a trend already mentioned above and known as "friend-shoring". This practice is a testament to the growing emphasis on supply chain resilience and national security. As nations and firms recalibrate their investment strategies, "friend-shoring" emerges as a way to reduce dependencies on potentially adversarial regions while securing economic ties with geopolitical partners.

Over the past decades, shifts in the global economy have fundamentally transformed its structure and dynamics. Accelerating rates of technological advancement, the expansion and consolidation of banks, corporations, and firms, and the deeper integration of global supply chains have contributed to the emergence of a unified global economy and financial system. In this context, foreign direct investment plays a significant role in driving economic integration and shaping international capital flows.

Whether driven by financial, technological, market, or geopolitical factors, the decisions of corporations and institutional investors are shaping the future of international trade and economic integration. By injecting capital, investors may require recipient countries and companies to strengthen investor protection and regulatory and compliance frameworks, as well as adopt corporate governance practices. More than just a capital flow, foreign direct investment intensifies competitive dynamics within domestic markets, reshapes industries, and pushes local firms to innovate to maintain their market positions.

1.3.2 What Compels Nations to Attract FDI and Seek Cooperation With Multinational Corporations?

FDI has been a dominant source of foreign capital inflows in developing economies. According to the UNCTAD World Investment Report, in 2022, developing economies attracted a record US$916 billion in FDI inflows, marking a historic peak. This occurred even as global FDI fell by 12 percent and FDI flows to developed economies declined by 37 percent, totaling US$378 billion.[14]

Understanding the motives behind FDI also offers a lens into how nations manage their growth, power, and integration into the global community. For recipient nations, the story is often nuanced. FDI frequently addresses critical gaps in funding and expertise that domestic resources can't fill. The benefits extend beyond capital flows, often fostering deeper cooperation between investors and domestic financial institutions, the establishment of new distribution networks, and the creation of entirely new business ventures—all of which support economic growth. The key motives for attracting FDI from a national perspective include:

- **Accelerating Economic Growth:** FDI serves as an additional source of capital accumulation in the productive/entrepreneurial form, which leads to the acceleration of a nation's economic growth.

- **Stimulate imports of other forms of capital**, such as portfolio investments and bank loans.
- **Dissimilate innovations and facilitate knowledge transfer**, including managerial expertise. Investments are typically accompanied by an influx of new technologies and management practices, which can significantly elevate local industries.
- **Fostering Trade and Market Integration:** FDI stimulates foreign trade flows through export and import operations of enterprises established through direct investments. Companies backed by foreign investors often become hubs for export and import operations, further embedding the recipient nation into the global economic network.
- **Strengthening the Foundations for Sustainable Growth**: FDI also acts as a stabilizing force in national development, particularly in economies vulnerable to fiscal or institutional volatility. Stable, sustained growth depends on long-term capital formation—something FDI can provide more reliably than volatile capital flows such as portfolio investment. Beyond contributing to the quantity of growth, FDI plays a critical role in improving its quality by supporting environmentally sustainable practices, reinforcing institutional capacity, and promoting socially inclusive development. These dimensions are increasingly seen as essential not only to attracting investment, but to ensuring FDI long-term impact. In many policy circles, this remains an underexplored aspect of FDI's long-term value.

In the current economic context, no economic system—whether in a developing nation or a transitioning economy—can achieve rapid growth without leveraging advanced technologies and innovations from developed nations or exporting its own products to them, as these nations hold substantial financial resources and demand. The pace and dynamics of the foreign investment process largely correlate with the dynamics and pace of the national economic development. The growing influence of corporations in both developed and developing countries underscores their significance in shaping the global investment landscape, particularly through strategic foreign direct investments.

While traditional factors—such as market size, economic growth, and population—remain crucial for attracting FDI, nontraditional factors like a favorable business environment and openness to trade are becoming increasingly important.

A conducive investment climate is the basic prerequisite to draw appeal for MNCs. This means macroeconomic stability and embracing measures like privatization, restructuring, and overhauling legal and tax frameworks to create an environment where investors feel secure, and opportunities can thrive at both the micro and institutional levels.

A nation's ability to attract and retain FDI hinges on its ability to create an investor-friendly investment climate. This encompasses more than just economic stability; it involves comprehensive reforms at the institutional level, including regulatory frameworks, tax policies, and infrastructure improvements. It is a complex economic category that expresses a set of political, macroeconomic, social, and cultural factors, as well as factors that inform the feasibility and reliability of investment decisions and, therefore, determine the propensity to invest. **Assessing the investment climate aims to deepen stakeholders' understanding of the subjective and objective conditions influencing investment decisions. Understanding the investment climate also means the ability to systematically organize and refine subjective perceptions of investment conditions and establish the fundamental opportunities for investment within a country's specific context while assessing associated risks.**

Countries that have managed to create **a favorable investment environment**—marked by political stability, transparent legal systems, and investor protections, as well as comprehensive information support for projects and investors, and active promotional activities such as exhibitions and investor presentations—have consistently attracted higher FDI inflows. During this period, many recipient nations implemented strategic measures to retain or enhance their investment appeal. In 2023 alone, according to the UNCTAD World Investment Report, 73 countries enacted 137 policy measures impacting FDI, with 72 percent favoring

investors. These **investor-favoring measures targeted four primary areas: facilitation** (39 percent), **incentives** (33 percent), **promotion** (14 percent), and **liberalization** (12 percent).[15]

However, the pace and distribution of FDI remain uneven, which is partly explained by a persistent preference for domestic over foreign investments, particularly in countries with large domestic markets or stable political environments, and is further characterized by two investment paradoxes: the home bias paradox and the Feldstein–Horioka paradox.

The home bias paradox suggests that multinational corporations in countries like the United States, Europe, and Japan prefer to invest in their domestic markets rather than international ones, and the share of domestic investments in the structure of their investment portfolios prevails. Information asymmetries about foreign markets and associated risks contribute to this bias.[16]

The Feldstein–Horioka paradox suggests a high correlation between national savings rates and domestic investment rates in many countries, which is counterintuitive in the context of a perfectly mobile global capital market—a scenario in which there should be little to no correlation between a country's savings and its investment, as savings would flow to where they can earn the highest return, regardless of national borders. However, this high correlation exists and indicates limited capital mobility, restricted by transaction costs, exchange-rate risks, information asymmetry, political risks, and regulations.[17]

1.3.3. The Behavioral Patterns of Donor Nations: How Do They Shape Global Investments?

Why do donor nations invest in and support outbound FDI? Far from being purely economic endeavors, outbound FDI serve as strategic instruments of statecraft, aligning MNCs with national priorities. These investments are a deliberate extension of state objectives designed to enhance economic competitiveness, secure critical resources, foster technological leadership, and protect geopolitical influence. By leveraging fiscal incentives, institutional frameworks, and policy alignment, donor nations ensure that FDI allows corporations to realize advantages and fortifies the nation's long-term strategic position. **FDI often entails expectations that** recipient countries will strengthen their regulatory and institutional frameworks, aligning with international standards. In return, recipient countries gain access not only to capital, but also to advanced technologies, managerial expertise, and integration into global value chains—though often at the cost of policy autonomy or increased exposure to external influence.

The strategic motivations for outbound FDI from a donor nation perspective can be distilled into four interconnected objectives:

1. **Economic Competitiveness and Market Leadership:** MNCs use outbound FDI to expand into new markets, achieve economies of scale, and gain early access to emerging technologies and talent pools. Governments amplify the impact of outbound FDI through strategic programs, including tax incentives, trade facilitation, and financial support. For instance, by providing financial and technical assistance, the U.S. Export-Import Bank plays a crucial role in enabling U.S. firms to overcome market barriers abroad. This deliberate alignment of corporate growth with national objectives reinforces the U.S. leadership in global capital flows and strengthens its strategic position in global markets. Similarly, Japan's JETRO facilitates investments in advanced manufacturing and robotics, reinforcing its competitive edge in global value chains.

2. **Geopolitical Influence:** FDI serves as a powerful geopolitical tool, reinforcing alliances and countering rival powers. Australia's Indo-Pacific investments exemplify this interplay, aligning economic growth with regional security objectives. Similarly, the United Kingdom's post-Brexit strategy prioritizes deepening ties with Commonwealth nations, strengthening its global influence through economic interdependence.

3. **Securing Critical Resources and Supply Chains:** Resource security is a cornerstone of outbound FDI strategies. Investments in rare earth minerals, energy supplies, and advanced materials ensure that donor nations maintain strategic control over essential supply chains. Canada and Australia actively promote investments in resource-rich regions to safeguard access to minerals and energy. Meanwhile, China has aggressively pursued investments in Africa and Latin America to

secure rare earth metals and agricultural commodities critical for its industrial base.

4. **Sector-Specific Leadership:** Nations encourage outbound FDI to secure a competitive edge and leadership position. For example, Germany channels outbound FDI into green tech and AI to maintain its industrial preeminence. China's "Made in China 2025" strategy illustrates how outbound investments are used to acquire strategic technologies, patents, and know-how. Australia's Modern Manufacturing Strategy, announced in 2020, focuses on building resilience in six priority sectors, including resources technology and critical minerals processing.

Some Forms of Strategic Alignment

As digital economies and security goals rise to the forefront, donor nations employ a sophisticated mix of fiscal tools, institutional support, and strategic policies to align corporate investments with state priorities:

- **Monetary Incentives**: Tax breaks, trade facilitation, and financial assistance lower barriers for MNCs.
- **State-Backed Insurance**: Programs mitigate risks in volatile markets, fostering confidence in high-potential but uncertain regions.
- **Long-Term Industrial Strategies:** Initiatives such as the United Kingdom's "Invest 2035" exemplify this approach by integrating business feedback to prioritize high-growth sectors and regions, thus fostering sustainable and inclusive economic expansion and reinforcing sectoral dominance. Japan's Ministry of Economy, Trade and Industry (METI) released the "New Industrial Structure Vision" in 2021, outlining strategies to enhance competitiveness in areas of digital transformation and green innovation. While there is no single document articulating "a modern American industrial strategy," the United States has outlined the nation's approach to industrial development and economic resilience through a series of legislative measures and policy statements. The approach emphasizes public investments to stimulate private sector innovation and long-term growth and promotes investment focus on sectors foundational to economic growth and national security.

At the same time, donor countries are exercising increased caution toward foreign investments in critical industries deemed essential for national and economic security. To address these concerns, nations have tightened regulations on foreign investments, with over half of global FDI flows now subject to national security screening mechanisms. These screening measures span a broad range of sectors, including defense and security, energy and utilities, critical infrastructure, automotive, financial services, health care and pharmaceuticals, electronics and semiconductors, media, communications and Internet services, and metals and mining (based on the UNCTAD World Investment Report 2024).

Screening of outward foreign direct investment (OFDI) has also been gaining momentum. While countries like China and Japan have longstanding frameworks to regulate their outbound investments, recent years have seen other donor nations implementing restrictions on capital outflows. For instance, in 2020, the United States introduced measures to monitor and regulate outbound FDI in sectors critical to national security. The European Commission proposed a framework in 2024 to oversee outbound investments in key strategic sectors, including advanced semiconductors and biotechnology.[18] The United States and the European Union (EU) work jointly to develop a standardized policy and approach to investment screening. Such moves reflect a broader trend among advanced economies to align their regulatory efforts in managing national security risks linked to cross-border investments.

The Future of Outbound FDI: As the global economy grows more tech-driven and geopolitically complex, outbound FDI will remain an essential instrument of global influence. From fostering innovation hubs to securing critical resources, donor nations are actively reshaping the investment landscape to ensure that their corporations—and their economies—remain resilient, adaptive, and competitive in a time of rapid and unprecedented change.

CHAPTER 2

Economic Models

2.1 The Interplay between Foreign Direct Investment and Economic Growth

Economic growth is a central objective of macroeconomic policy, a crucial economic goal for every country, and one of the most significant social issues that consistently draws the attention of both economists and policy makers. Growth is measured by the increase in gross domestic product (GDP, national income, and gross national product (GNP), and it determines everything from living standards to a nation's power in global trade.

In essence, **economic growth ensures that real output (GDP) grows faster than population**. The **key goals and objectives** set by states in the process of ensuring economic growth typically include:

- **Improving living standards, reducing social inequality, and reducing poverty**;
- **Strengthening the nation's economic power** by expanding production, increasing GDP, and increasing the nation's share in global GDP and world trade;
- **Achieving technological competitiveness** through the continuous adoption of innovative technologies.

Understanding the essence of economic growth requires an in-depth analysis of the key factors that drive it. Traditionally, these factors include the following: availability and quality of natural resources, efficiency of capital investments, size and skill level of labor force, accumulation of capital stock, and technological advancements. Table 2.1 illustrates the respective contributions of labor, fixed capital, and technological progress to global economic growth, offering a data-driven view on these factors.

Table 2.1 Contribution of key economic growth factors in major global economies

Country	Period	Average annual GDP growth rate (%)	Labor force (% of total)	Fixed capital (% of total)	Technological progress (% of total)
United States	2001–2010	2.5	36	32	32
	2011–2020	2.2	31.8	29.5	38.7
	2021–2024	2.5	32	28	40
EU-27	2001–2010	1.9	15.8	42.1	42.1
	2011–2020	1.7	11.8	41.2	47
	2021–2024	1.8	11	35	54
China	2001–2010	10.5	26.7	42.9	30.4
	2011–2020	6.7	22.4	52.2	25.4
	2021–2024	5.3	24.5	50.9	24.6
United Kingdom	2001–2010	2.4	33.3	33.3	33.4
	2011–2020	1.9	26.3	36.8	36.9
	2021–2024	1.7	23.5	35.3	41.2
Japan	2001–2010	1.4	28.6	57.1	14.3
	2011–2020	1	20	60	20
	2021–2024	1.4	14.3	39.7	46
Singapore	2001–2010	5.7	26.3	40.4	33.3
	2011–2020	3.6	25	38.9	36.1
	2021–2024	3.2	25	37.5	37.5

Source: IMF, World Bank, and the 2024 World Investment Report by UNCTAD.

An analysis of this data suggests that the contribution of technological progress to economic growth has been steadily increasing across developed economies over the past two decades. Technological progress—defined as the practical application of accumulated knowledge and information in traditional production and intangible forms—has noticeably contributed to economic growth. Yet it is important not to discount the ongoing relevance of traditional growth drivers.

Over the past two decades, the impact of labor's contribution to GDP growth has modestly declined, making it the smallest among the three primary components of growth. Technological advancement has largely offset this decline, without diminishing the continued importance of capital investment. Given the central importance of both technological advancement and fixed capital investment, high-tech investment is regarded as a critical driver of global competitiveness and long-term economic performance.

Historically, FDI has long been a contributor to economic infrastructure development. For instance, in the mid-nineteenth century, British capital played a significant role in enabling large-scale investments in the United States and Canada, facilitating the construction of vital rail networks. This development catalyzed economic growth by increasing the welfare of farmers, increasing the value of agricultural land, and spurring the rise of import-substituting industries such as steel production.

Today, the central question is not whether foreign direct investment drives growth, but under what conditions it serves as a catalyst for national development—and when it becomes a source of risk.

Advocates of policies that favor openness to FDI argue that foreign capital effectively bridges domestic resource gaps, providing a crucial influx of capital that drives further growth and development—a point explored in the previous chapter. They emphasize that beyond capital, FDI often brings technology, management expertise, and enhanced business standards, creating multifaceted benefits for economic growth.

Critics, however, warn of risks and adverse implications for host economies. Commonly cited concerns include the disproportionate influence of multinational corporations (MNCs) over national policymaking, the overexploitation of national resources, tendencies to bypass environmental and labor regulations, and an overreliance on foreign suppliers, which introduces additional supply chain vulnerabilities. Yet, even among critics, few deny that FDI, properly managed, can make a powerful contribution to a nation's prosperity.

In our view, **the dynamics of economic growth are heavily influenced by the flow and quality of FDI. This suggests the need for both theoretical and empirical research to explore the relationships and interdependencies between FDI and economic growth in capital-receiving countries**. A logical starting point for such research is to examine existing theories of economic growth, with a focus on the role and significance of FDI within these frameworks.

The theory of economic growth began to take shape in the 1930s and 1940s, driven by the desire to understand the factors that lead to long-term, balanced growth. These theories aimed (1) to explain the drivers of long-term economic growth, focusing on factors such as capital, labor, and technological progress, and (2) to identify the conditions (such as savings rates, investment in capital, labor productivity, and technological innovation) necessary for balanced and sustainable growth.

The **foundational work** in this field was laid by the British economist **R. Harrod** and the American economist **E. Domar**, who, in their models, relied on a fixed ratio between the values of labor and capital used in production.[19,20] However, these early models did not account for changes in the capitalization of labor and/or the impact of technological progress, limiting their ability to accurately depict economic growth.

In the 1950s and 1960s, Nobel laureate **Robert Solow** advanced the theory by introducing **a variable capital–labor ratio and a parameter for technological progress.**[21] Solow's work demonstrated that technological progress was responsible for at least half of the increase in output per worker in the United States. His neoclassical growth model became the dominant framework in economic literature until the mid-1970s when **Nicholas Kaldor** and **Joan Robinson** challenged this approach.[22,23] While their models included a **broader range of economic growth factors** and were more closely **aligned with the complexities of real economic life**, they lacked the precision and clarity of the neoclassical models.

A new phase in the development of economic growth theory emerged in the 1980s and 1990s. **A new growth theory** incorporated the **effects of imperfect competition and variations in profit rates** and, most importantly, treated **innovation and technological progress as an endogenous factor**—meaning it was generated from within the economic system itself. **Paul Romer** and **Robert Lucas** formalized **economic and mathematical models proposing the hypothesis that key production and technological innovations are endogenous, driven by investments in scientific and technological progress (STP) and human capital.**[24,25]

2.2 Unlocking Economic Growth: Four Essential Models You Need to Know

Can we unlock the formula for continuous, sustainable growth—or is there a perfect equation for economic prosperity?

Having considered the fundamentals of the history and theory of FDI, we will now explore the most essential frameworks that seek to explain the direct and indirect relationships between economic growth and the dynamics of FDI. The **Solow Model**[26], **Leontief's Input–Output Model**, **James Markusen's Knowledge–Capital Model**, and the **Welfens– Jasinski Model** each offer a different angle into economic growth, trade interdependencies, and the movement of capital across borders. The Solow Model laid the foundation for modern growth theory, introducing the concept of exogenous technological progress as the central driver of long-term economic growth. Leontief's Input-Output Model has been used to analyze sectoral interdependencies. James Markusen's Knowledge–Capital Model offers a theoretical framework for understanding the behavior of multinational firms, including how and why they invest abroad. Finally, the Welfens–Jasinski Model addresses international macroeconomic dynamics, focusing on topics such as capital flows, FDI, and the role of technological progress in economic integration.

1. **The Solow Model of Economic Growth:** Developed by economist Robert Solow in the 1950s, it is also known as the Solow–Swan Model. This foundational framework explains long-term economic growth through the key drivers of capital accumulation, labor force expansion, and technological progress.

   According to this model, the rate of economic growth is expressed as follows:

   $$g_y = g_A + \alpha g_k$$

Where:
- g_y is the growth rate of output (GDP) per worker;
- g_A is the rate of technological progress;
- g_k is the growth rate of capital per worker;
- α is the output elasticity of capital (a constant that reflects how much output responds to a change in capital).

The core equation of the Solow Model expresses **the relationship between savings, population growth, depreciation, and capital accumulation**. The fundamental equation, also known as the capital accumulation equation, is:

$$\Delta k = s{\cdot}f(k) - (n + \delta){\cdot}k,$$

where k is capital per worker (capital–labor ratio), Δk is a change in capital per worker over time, s is a savings rate, $f(k)$ is an output per worker as a function of capital per worker (typically represented as $f(k) = k^{\alpha}$, where α is the output elasticity of capital), n is a population growth rate, and δ is a depreciation rate.

In this equation:

- $s{\cdot}f(k)$ represents the amount of output saved and invested in new capital;
- $(n + \delta){\cdot}k$ accounts for the effects of population growth and depreciation on existing capital stock.

The model seeks to determine the steady-state level of capital per worker, denoted as k^*, where $\Delta k = 0$. At this point, the capital stock per worker remains constant over time. This steady state occurs when the amount of new capital generated by savings and investment equals the amount of capital lost to depreciation and population growth. In the steady-state, the equation simplifies to:

$$s{\cdot}f(k^*) = (n + \delta){\cdot}k$$

In the extended version of the Solow Model, technological progress (g) is introduced, which shifts the production function upward over time and leads to higher output per worker. In this case, the steady-state equation becomes:

$$s{\cdot}f(k^*) = (n + \delta + g){\cdot}k$$

where g is a rate of technological progress. In the extended version of the Solow Model, the rate of technological progress, denoted as *g*, shifts the production function over time, resulting in increased output per worker due to technological progress. In other words, **technological progress drives long-term growth by increasing productivity**.

The Solow Model demonstrates how economies converge to a steady-state level of capital per worker and output per worker based on their savings rates, population growth rates, and depreciation rates. Moreover, **it highlights that while savings and capital accumulation are important for growth, technological progress is essential for sustaining long-term growth**.

Reflecting the dynamics outlined in the Solow Growth Model, a nation's economic growth can be classified into two key phases:

Accelerated Capital Accumulation Phase: This initial phase is characterized by accelerated growth due to an increase in the capital productivity of labor through the attraction of FDI. For instance, China has demonstrated substantial growth through enhanced capital per worker, leveraging external capital to boost productivity and stimulate expansion. The capital accumulation leads to improvements in output but eventually faces diminishing marginal returns.

Sustainable Growth Phase: Once an economy reaches a steady-state level of capital per worker, future growth relies on technological progress. According to the Solow Model, long-term GDP growth in this phase is primarily driven by technological innovation and population growth, rather than continued capital accumulation. Economic development at this stage focuses on qualitative improvements in FDI, with an emphasis on enhancing technological sophistication and operational efficiency. This marks a transition from extensive growth (driven by capital) to intensive growth (driven by innovation), underscoring the critical role of technology in sustaining long-term economic growth.

This fundamental model emphasizes that capital accumulation alone is insufficient for sustained growth due to diminishing returns. Instead, technological progress is essential to achieving continuous growth in per capita output. While the Solow Model does not explicitly factor in

FDI, FDI indirectly influences the capital–output ratio in both phases—accelerated capital accumulation and sustainable growth.

As we navigate an era of unprecedented technological acceleration, one question persists: Where does innovation begin, and who will lead its future?

Solow's insights laid the foundation for understanding the symbiotic relationship between public investment and private innovation. While technological advancement is recognized as the central driver of economic growth, it often emerges as an external factor—one that markets alone may not generate efficiently. Solow, renowned for his contributions to growth theory, served as a senior economist on President Kennedy's Council of Economic Advisers from 1961 to 1963, advising on macroeconomic policies, employment, and growth policies.

Solow has long argued that governments are uniquely positioned to address market inefficiencies, especially where private sector incentives fall short—such as in long-term, high-risk investments. His writings and interviews frequently mention the importance of public investment, especially in areas such as research and development (R&D), and also education, where private incentives may be weak. In his view, while the private sector plays a vital role in applying new technologies, the public sector creates the necessary conditions for innovation by investing in foundational research and offering incentives for private enterprises to follow suit. This view is reinforced by subsequent economists who expanded on his growth model.

As we stand at the intersection of public and private forces shaping the future of innovation, one thing becomes clear: Sustained technological leadership will depend not only on market dynamics but also on strategic investment and public-private partnerships PPPs. Governments, according to Solow, are in a position to make strategic investments in education, research and development R&D, and infrastructure—essential elements that create an environment conducive to technological progress. The private sector will transform these foundations into marketable innovations, thus driving innovation commercialization. Together, this synergy ensures that businesses remain competitive in a rapidly evolving landscape, with public-private partnership (PPPs) serving as catalysts. Historically, PPPs and government incentives have already spurred technological advancements in energy, biotechnology, and information technology, and this approach can be applied to other sectors.

2. Leontief's Input–Output Model: The 1930s Tool That Still Drives Economic Planning Today

Wassily Leontief's Input–Output (I-O) Model, first developed in the 1930s, drastically changed how economists and policy makers analyze the interdependencies between sectors of an economy. By mapping the flow of goods and services between industries, the I-O model allows us to measure how the output of one industry serves as the input for another. This highlights how sectors depend on each other for inputs and outputs and illustrates the deep interconnectedness of industries within a national economy.

The core idea of Leontief's model is that the economy can be represented as a system of linear equations, showing how much each sector consumes from and produces for other sectors. These relationships are captured through an input–output matrix, where each element quantifies how much output from one sector is used as input by another, offering a deeper understanding of sectoral dependencies and external demands. The model is expressed as:

$$X = (I - A)^{-1} D$$

Where:
- X is the total output;
- A is the input–output coefficient matrix (how much input is required from each sector);
- D is the final demand (external demand);
- I is the identity matrix.

This equation allows economists to calculate the total production required across industries to meet both internal and external demand.

Leontief's model became one of the foundational tools for understanding how changes in demand in one sector can affect the broader economy and predict inefficiencies by showing whether certain sectors produce more than is required to meet demand.

One of the greatest strengths of the I-O model is that it is grounded in real data. All parameters of the Leontief model are easy to estimate and apply in various ways. National statistical agencies and international organizations collect the necessary data, enabling highly accurate economic modeling. This makes the model a powerful forecasting tool that governments have used for decades to predict the effects of policy changes or economic shocks

The model also evolved into a powerful planning tool for assessing the parameters necessary to achieve specific economic growth targets. One of its key innovations is its ability to quantify relationships between sectors, making it easier to analyze how shifts—such as surges in demand or supply chain disruptions—impact overall economic performance.

The Input–Output Model: A Postwar Solution with Modern Applications

Faced with the challenge of transitioning from war economies to peacetime growth, governments required an effective decision-making tool. The I-O model quickly became indispensable for economic planning during the postwar recovery period. For example, during World War II, the U.S. government utilized the I-O model to forecast postwar economic demand, particularly for key resources like steel. This foresight helped guide critical resource allocation decisions, contributing to a smoother economic transition and helping to avert a postwar recession.

The I-O model has been invaluable in assessing the impact of economic crises. During the oil shocks of the 1970s, for example, the model was used to analyze how rising oil prices would affect different industries, from transportation to manufacturing. The model's predictive power helped governments and businesses prepare for and mitigate the effects of such shocks. It became a useful tool for understanding how a change in consumer demand or an increase in raw material costs could ripple through the economy.

How did a tool born in the pre-digital age remain so powerful in a world dominated by AI and real-time analytics?

The answer lies in the model's foundational ability to map interdependencies between industries, both locally and globally. It revolutionized the way we understand economies now as a system of interdependence, where no industry functions in isolation.

What is truly compelling about the I-O model is its versatility. Initially developed for national economies, it now powers insights across global trade, supply chains, climate impact studies, and disaster management. Its adaptability to evolving economic realities—whether addressing global interdependencies or foreign investment planning—ensures it remains a trusted tool for policy makers and business leaders.

When planning budgets or predicting economic trends, ministries of finance still use the I-O model to simulate the effects of policy changes. This is not just a theoretical exercise; the model provides real-time, data-driven insights into how different industries interact and depend on each other.

With environmental sustainability climbing to the top of corporate and governmental agendas, the I-O model has found new applications in Environmental Input-Output (EIO) analysis. By calculating how industries contribute to carbon emissions, the model helps policy makers design targeted environmental regulations and shape decisions on green policies and carbon taxation.

Cities and regions worldwide use I-O models for regional and urban planning. If a city plans to invest in new infrastructure, this model can predict which local industries will benefit the most and how the changes will cascade through the local economy. This intricate mapping of cause and effect keeps the model relevant.

Beyond governments, corporations and industries can also reap the benefits. The model's capacity for dissecting global trade relations makes it a powerful forecasting tool for supply chain analysis. The COVID-19 pandemic demonstrated just how fragile global supply chains can be, with disruptions in one country affecting industries in another. The I-O model traces these connections, revealing the hidden intricacies of trade interdependence and allowing businesses to better manage risk.

Disaster management is another unexpected yet practical application of the I-O model. After a natural disaster strikes, policy makers use this tool to estimate the ripple effects on industries that weren't directly affected. For instance, a flood in a tech manufacturing hub could severely impact car production halfway across the globe. With the I-O model, governments and companies can better prepare for and recover from these economic shocks.

From the United Nations to the World Bank, the I-O model remains relevant in shaping global economic policies. The UN incorporates it into its System of National Accounts (SNA), providing nations with a framework for compiling consistent and comparable macroeconomic statistics. The Organization for Economic Co-operation and Development (OECD) leverages I-O tables to analyze global trade flows and productivity across nations. The World Bank uses it as a forecasting tool and to study the impact of investments in different regions or industries.

Modeling FDI Dynamics: Developed and Developing Economies

The model can also be adapted to assess the impact of FDI flows on the long-term economic development of national economies by analyzing the interaction between two groups of countries—developed and developing—connected through the flow of production investments from developed to developing nations.

For developed countries, two principles can be applied:

- **The Multiplier Principle:** Expressed as $I(t) = sY(t)$, where Y represents output (GNP), I is the volume of investment in developed countries at time t, and s is the rate of accumulation or investment multiplier.
- The Multiplier Principle explains how an initial investment stimulates broader economic activity by triggering successive rounds of spending and production, thus amplifying its overall impact on aggregate demand.

- **The Accelerator Principle:** Expressed as $Y(t) = I(t)/b$, where b is the capital–output ratio or investment accelerator.
- The Accelerator Principle highlights the dynamic relationship between output growth and investment. It shows how businesses expand capital spending in response to rising demand, thus creating a feedback loop that accelerates economic growth.

Combining the principles of the multiplier and accelerator allows us to obtain the final differential equation describing the dynamics of output in the group of developed countries:

$$Y(t) = U(0)e^{(s/b)t}$$

Where $U(0)$ is the initial output, s/b is the ratio of the multiplier to the accelerator, influencing the growth rate.

Capital Export Equation: Captures the concept of capital transfer from developed to developing countries, assuming a constant share of output, where h is the constant share of GNP transferred as capital from developed countries. The formula for exported capital H(t) is presented as follows:

$$H(t) = hY(0)e^{(s/b)t}$$

For developing countries, a similar correlation can be derived:
Modified Multiplier Principle for Developing Countries, where the formula for investments in developing countries is expressed as:

$$I^*(t) = s^*Y^*(t) + h(0)e^{(s/b)t},$$

The formula is valid under the assumption that investments in developing countries are driven by both domestic factors and external capital inflows. It combines domestic and imported investments denoted by $h(0)$.

The Accelerator Principle is expressed as:

$$Y^*(t) = I^*(t)/b^* \tag{2.1}$$

By combining these principles, the model describes the output dynamics in developing countries:

$$Y^*(t) = \left[Y^*(0) - \frac{H(0)}{b^*(s/b - s^*/b^*)} \right] e^{(s^*/b^*)t} + \frac{H(0)}{b^*(s/b - s^*/b^*)} e^{(s/b)t} \tag{2.2}$$

This model demonstrates that **economic growth in developing countries is directly tied to the growth rate in developed countries and the initial amount of capital exported from them.**

The model has certain **limitations, particularly its assumption of homogeneity in imported capital**, which overlooks the fact that the composition and quality of capital can be as critical as its volume. Additionally, **it assumes that both domestic and foreign investments are equally effective, which may not hold true in varied economic environments or sectors.**

3. How FDI Fuels Economic Growth: Insights from the Welfens–Jasinski Model

Rooted in the production function framework and expanded upon Solow's growth model, the Welfens–Jasinski Model integrates FDI as a central driver of national economic growth. This model offers a nuanced understanding of how foreign capital interacts with domestic resources, labor, and technological progress, providing a strategic lens through which policy makers can assess FDI's long-term economic impact. Specifically, it explores **how foreign capital combined with domestic resources contributes to overall Gross Domestic Product GDP or Gross National Product GNP growth.**

The Welfens–Jasinski production function describing economic growth in the recipient country is:

$$Y(t) = [K(t) + H(t)]^{\beta} [L(t)] \ e^{(1 - \beta)zt}$$

Where:

- $Y(t)$ represents **output** (GDP or GNP) at time t;
- $K(t)$ is the fixed capital of **domestic origin**;
- $H(t)$ is the fixed capital of **foreign origin**;
- $L(t)$ is the number of employees in the national economy;
- z is the rate of scientific and technological progress **(STP)**;
- β is a statistically estimated parameter that governs the elasticity of output to capital inputs.

In this model, Welfens and Jasinski identify foreign fixed capital with accumulated FDI. Economic growth is driven by the combined contributions of domestic and foreign capital, alongside labor and technological progress. FDI represented as foreign fixed capital (H) is combined with local fixed assets (K) to generate output. At the same time, the rate of technical progress (z) in their interpretation depends on four parameters: (1) amount of accumulated knowledge within the economy, (2) relative value of imported intermediate goods compared to total output, (3) degree of development of market institutions that facilitate economic growth, and (4) value of exports, which contributes to productivity and competitiveness.

The Welfens–Jasinski model generally treats domestic and foreign capital as functionally similar inputs in the production process and recognizes that foreign capital can be particularly beneficial in transition economies due to technology transfer and managerial know-how. In reality, the efficiency of foreign capital may vary depending on factors such as institutional quality and the absorptive capacity of the host economy. Additionally, the model treats the rate of economic growth as exogenous, meaning it does not account for feedback loops where investment itself may influence the pace of growth. These limitations open the door for further research and innovation in economic modeling, although the model does offer nonetheless important strategic insight for policy makers, such as the importance of nurturing a favorable investment climate that can attract and efficiently utilize FDI. By developing strong market institutions, investing in education and research to boost knowledge accumulation, and ensuring that domestic industries are competitive globally, nations can maximize the benefits of FDI and stimulate long-term economic growth.

The Welfens–Jasinski Model highlights FDI as a pivotal driver of economic growth, particularly for developing and transition economies. By recognizing the transformative role of foreign capital—especially when paired with the transfer of knowledge and technology—the model underscores FDI's capacity to boost productivity and unlock a nation's economic potential.

4. The New Rules of Global Investment: Capitalizing on the Knowledge–Capital Interplay

Markusen's Knowledge–Capital Model helps policy makers and economists understand the intricate role of knowledge in forming FDI patterns. The model focuses on the interplay between knowledge and capital as the core driver behind MNC decisions to invest abroad. It offers a comprehensive view of how firms decide where to locate production, how to best capitalize on knowledge assets, and how to leverage the unique advantages of each individual country.

Unlike traditional models that focus on either replicating production across multiple countries (horizontal FDI) or splitting production processes to benefit from cost advantages (vertical FDI), Markusen's model shows that MNCs pursue both strategies simultaneously. The horizontal aspect emphasizes creating production sites in similar high-income economies to avoid trade barriers and gain proximity to customers, while vertical FDI highlights the cost-saving measures gained by shifting labor-intensive stages to developing countries.

This hybrid approach illustrates how MNCs view their global operations and/or executive location strategy through FDI. Firms tend to locate their knowledge—or capital-intensive activities—such as R&D and management—in countries with skilled labor forces while positioning labor-intensive production in lower-cost regions, thus maximizing the productivity and cost-efficiency of the entire value chain.

Countries with similar economic structures are often motivated to invest abroad through horizontal FDI. Having similar factor endowments (such as labor, capital, technology, and knowledge), they tend to both invest in and receive FDI in the same industries, generating intra-industry trade where similar goods and services are exported and imported between economies.

The model builds on Paul Romer's premise that knowledge is a nonrivalrous resource. Multinational firms with significant knowledge-based assets, such as technological know-how, managerial expertise, or brand recognition, can efficiently exploit these assets across multiple locations and transfer them at minimal cost. The low marginal cost of transferring knowledge means that it is profitable for these firms to establish operations in other knowledge-advanced economies with similar factor endowments where the demand for their products is high. Moreover, MNCs rely on intangible assets (such as intellectual property, brand equity, and managerial skills) in recipient countries to establish foreign operations. Since these firms do not need significantly different inputs (like low-cost labor or raw materials), their FDIs are driven by the desire to exploit existing expertise in multiple markets. This leads to both countries simultaneously becoming a source and destination for FDI, creating a network of multinational activities across similar economies.

Advanced economies often engage in FDI to acquire strategic assets such as new technologies, R&D capabilities, or access to skilled labor markets, tapping into each other's scientific and innovation hubs and fostering cross-border mergers and acquisitions. This is especially common in knowledge-intensive sectors such as pharmaceuticals, technology, and finance, where firms benefit from acquiring complementary intellectual capital. For instance, a U.S. tech firm may acquire a cutting-edge AI startup in the United Kingdom, while a British pharmaceutical company may invest in acquiring R&D capabilities in the United States.

By focusing on the behavior of multinational corporations, the model helps to understand how the FDI activities of these firms lead to technology diffusion, productivity gains, and increased specialization of a nation. The Knowledge–Capital Model provides insights into how multinational firms optimize their global operations by balancing investments in knowledge-intensive hubs with those in cost-effective production hubs. This gives policy makers and business leaders a framework to leverage this knowledge–capital synergy and position themselves to ensure technological and global competitiveness. On the policy front, governments can use the model's findings to attract FDI by creating environments conducive to knowledge- and technology-intensive investments or by channeling FDI into labor-intensive production through tax incentives, infrastructure investments, and favorable trade regimes.

As a closing thought, we consider insights from the IMF's econometric models—sophisticated frameworks designed to evaluate a nation's growth potential.

Using a comprehensive dataset spanning 208 countries over four decades, IMF experts analyzed the factors influencing economic growth. Their findings are unequivocal: Among the many variables assessed, the share of FDI in GDP and the share of total investment in GDP emerged as the most impactful drivers of growth. The data reveal that a 1-percentage-point increase in the share of domestic investment in GDP adds approximately 1.63 percentage points to a country's economic growth rate. Similarly, a 1-percentage-point rise in the share of FDI in

GDP contributes about 6.5 percentage points to growth—underscoring the strong sensitivity of economic growth to FDI.

The study highlights that the level of a country's economic development and growth is, to a large extent, determined by FDI. FDI has consistently proven to be a catalyst for economic growth, particularly in emerging and developing markets. Qualitative aspects of investment—particularly in knowledge-intensive sectors—are seen as key to sustaining growth.

CHAPTER 3

Unlocking Potential: How Transition Economies Used FDI to Drive Growth and Global Integration

The next essential step in understanding how FDI fuels economic growth in host countries is to examine the experiences of transition economies that have leveraged FDI as a driver of development and economic growth. In this analysis, we will focus on the case studies of several key groups of countries with transition economies:

- **Central and Eastern Europe (CEE)**
- **Post-Soviet States**
- **China**

Studying these regions is particularly relevant, as they have undergone significant economic transitions. Each has evolved from a nonmarket economy through periods of isolation from foreign investors to phases of privatization, liberalization, and economic reform aimed at integration into the global supply chain and world economy. The individual countries concerned have successfully navigated many typical challenges: regulatory overhaul, financial instability, and institutional restructuring. In their quest for WTO acceptance, these transitioning economies carried out substantial commitments, aligning their economic and trade policies with global standards, leading to economic growth and global influence in ways that were not obvious or anticipated. Their experiences provide valuable lessons in attracting FDI and harnessing it as a critical engine of growth in transitional settings.

3.1 How FDI Transformed Central Europe: Lessons from Poland, the Czech Republic, and Slovakia

The Czech Republic, Poland, and Slovakia have emerged as standout success stories in Central and Eastern Europe (CEE), leading the region in attracting FDI. All three countries have drawn substantial FDI flows, particularly from EU investors, due to a combination of factors: proximity to the EU investors' own markets, skilled yet affordable labor, and well-developed infrastructure. For investors, privatization of state-owned enterprises, expansion of home markets, and enhanced profitability made the entire CEE region an attractive destination.

Initially, the CEE region was virtually untouched by FDI, but it quickly caught up with the EU and other markets. What began as an underinvested market quickly evolved into a stable and high-potential economic region, driven by a focused pursuit of FDI to fuel its transition.

Its current stability and great potential can be explained by the fact that the market was oriented toward the search for FDI: In 1995, the ratio of FDI to GDP in the region was 5.3 percent; by 2005, this figure increased to 20.9 percent, which is not much lower than the world average of 22.5 percent. This positive trend continued, with the FDI-to-GDP ratio reaching almost 25 percent by 2014. The upward trajectory continued, and, by 2024, the FDI-to-GDP ratio in the region had grown to around 28 percent, reflecting sustained investor confidence and the region's deep integration into the global economy.

This success was not coincidental; it resulted from deliberate and strategic actions taken by CEE countries, particularly through the **effective use of Investment Promotion Agencies (IPAs)**.

CzechInvest, established in 1992, actively promoted the Czech Republic as an attractive destination for foreign investors. By educating investors on the country's strategic advantages—such as its skilled labor force, proximity to EU markets, and favorable investment environment—CzechInvest facilitated the entry of high-value industries such as high-tech, automotive, and electronics. This positioned the Czech Republic as a major player in European manufacturing, particularly in the automotive sector, where it has become a hub for both production and innovation. CzechInvest's comprehensive support—including site selection assistance, regulatory guidance, and post-investment services—enhanced the ease of doing business (a key consideration for foreign investors) and propelled the growth of high-value sectors.

Similarly, Poland's Investment and Trade Agency (PAIH) facilitated seamless entry into the Polish economy by offering regulatory guidance, assisting with site selection, and fostering strategic partnerships with local stakeholders. PAIH positioned Poland as a highly attractive destination for FDI. This work translated into significant FDI inflows, which modernized Poland's industrial base and supported the economy's integration into global supply chains. It transformed Poland from a post-communist economy into one of Europe's most dynamic and rapidly growing markets.

Beyond the role of IPAs, the CEE region works toward alignment with global trade agreements, notably the WTO, and its acceptance later into the EU strengthened its investment appeal. WTO membership signaled full integration into the global trading system, while EU accession provided access to the single market and solidified economic and strategic ties with Western Europe. This integration was underpinned by significant regulatory reforms, including the strengthening of property rights, competition laws, and corporate governance, which further boosted investor confidence.

The **strategic use of Bilateral Investment Treaties (BITs)** added another layer of protection and reassurance for foreign investors. Poland, Slovakia, and the Czech Republic, all signed numerous BITs with their major investment partners, including the United States, Germany, and the United Kingdom. These treaties provided solid legal protections for investors, including such provisions as full protection and security for foreign investments, fair and equitable treatment, and protection against expropriation and offered dispute settlement mechanisms, often including international arbitration. Additionally, BITs ensured the free transfer of capital, including profits, dividends, and returns, out of the host country without undue restrictions or delays.

All these agreements and treaties were designed to offer foreign investors protection and establish a stable and predictable legal environment—key components of a favorable investment climate.

What is a strategic lesson from the CEE experience? A **conducive investment climate** is the required condition to draw appeal for multinational corporations MNCs. This means **macroeconomic stability** and embracing measures like **privatization, restructuring,** and **overhauling legal and tax frameworks** to create an environment where investors feel secure and opportunities thus can thrive. **FDI attraction is not a passive process—it requires deliberate, multilayered strategies.**

What is next? Countries that consistently demonstrate strong economic performance and maintain stable—or, ideally, growing— consumer purchasing power are consistently able to attract substantial foreign investment. A stable macroeconomic environment is a basic prerequisite for drawing in FDI. By prioritizing macroeconomic stability and aligning policy with global standards, transitioning economies can effectively position themselves as attractive destinations for FDI.

All three countries have successfully maintained GDP growth rates of at least 3 percent while reducing inflation. In Poland, and particularly in the Czech Republic, inflation remains near 0 percent—a remarkable achievement in the current economic climate. In terms of public debt, all three countries managed a debt-to-GDP ratio of around 40 percent, and the pace of debt reduction places them ahead of many their EU counterparts.

Since gaining independence, Slovakia has initially lagged behind the Czech Republic and Poland in GDP per capita, GDP growth, and inflation. However, in recent years, Slovakia has been steadily closing this gap, leading in annual GDP growth and, in some years, outperforming Poland in FDI inflows per capita. Privatization, alongside the anticipated EU accession, has been a critical driver of increased foreign investment.

This economic momentum was not just a reflection of the expansion of the EU; it was also a result of prudent policy signaling to global investors that these nations are deliberately focused on growth and actively creating opportunities.

One of the most compelling examples of FDI's impact can be seen in **Poland's** economic story—a nation that, between 1998 and 2005, shifted from decline to resurgence, driven by strategic reforms and an influx of capital (Figure 3.1).

As illustrated in the chart above, Poland's economy experienced a decline in investment growth starting in 1998, which worsened in 2002 and 2003, as growth rates turned negative. Privatization-related FDI slowed down between 1998 and 2003, whereas economic uncertainty in Poland, related to structural reforms and inconsistent policies, also contributed to

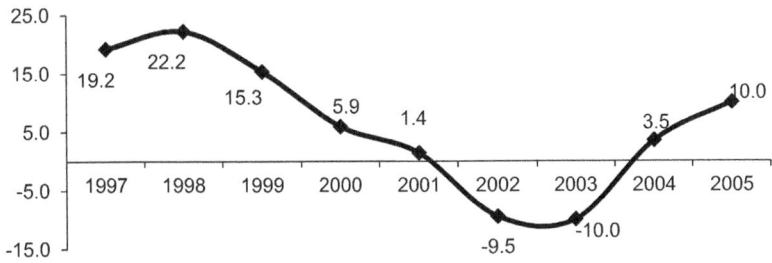

Figure 3.1 Growth rates of foreign investment in Poland's economy—percentage compared to the previous year

further declines in investment. However, 2004 marked a turning point, with Poland's accession to the EU triggering a resurgence in foreign investment, particularly from Eurozone countries. Investment increased by 3.5 percent that year, and this upward momentum continued into 2005, with growth reaching nearly 10 percent compared to the previous year. A substantial increase in FDI has been instrumental in revitalizing Poland's macroeconomic environment and fueling its sustained economic growth.

Table 3.1 presents the sectoral distribution of FDI in Poland, indicating the proportion of FDI allocated to each economic sector.

Poland's focus on investment-friendly policies, its proactive engagement with investors, and a revitalized privatization effort significantly contributed to its economic transformation, particularly in the 2000s. Between 2004 and 2014, Poland experienced a noticeable rise in FDI, largely driven by its EU accession. The most significant growth occurred in high-tech industries such as electrical engineering, telecommunications equipment, and automotive manufacturing, where investment surged by 40 percent, significantly enhancing the competitiveness of Polish-manufactured products. The automotive sector, in particular, saw a remarkable 60 percent annual increase in investment, attracting global automotive giants, with leading automakers such as Fiat, General Motors, Daewoo, and Volkswagen making significant investments. Poland became a hub for automotive production in Europe, benefiting from its skilled workforce and favorable logistics. Additionally, Poland's large consumer market—with over 38 million people—has attracted substantial FDI, particularly in the food industry, driven by the growing demand within the country and the country's strategic position within Europe.

Table 3.1 Structure of FDI in Poland by economic sector

Sectors of the Economy	2004–2014 (%)	2014–2024 (%)
1. Industry	30.0	28.0
2. Financial services	24.5	22.0
3. Electricity, gas, water	5.0	6.0
4. Wholesale and retail trade, transport repair	13.0	12.5
5. IT sector	7.5	10.0
6. Transportation, storage, and communication	8.5	9.0
7. Real estate, lease, and entrepreneurship	3.0	5.0
8. Development and extraction of mineral resources	0.5	1.0
9. Construction	3.5	3.8
10. Social security	2.5	1.5
11. Hotels and restaurants	1.8	2.0
12. Health care	4.0	5.5
13. Agriculture	0.2	0.2

In contrast, the market services sector faced some challenges, with investment in trade falling by 5 percent, transport and communications by 9 percent, and financial services by nearly 34 percent. The uneven distribution of capital reveals untapped potential and highlights the need for more targeted strategies to unlock growth across the entire economy.

During this period, the primary sources of FDI were Germany, the United States, France, and the United Kingdom, with capital inflows primarily targeting Poland's industrial base, logistics networks, and renewable energy sector. These sustained investments have played a decisive role in shaping Poland's economic trajectory and strengthening its position within European value chains.

Moreover, Poland's investment landscape has matured considerably, marked by a growing share of reinvested earnings within total FDI inflows. By 2017, reinvested profits surpassed net new inflows by approximately 14 percent, reflecting growing investor confidence and long-term commitment. Between 2010 and 2018, the total value of assets held by foreign-owned enterprises surged by 70%, helping to create a market now exceeding US$415 billion in asset value. On average, the capital invested annually in Poland grew by about 7 percent, outpacing the

Central and Eastern European (CEE) average of less than 5 percent. By the close of 2019, the cumulative value of FDI in Poland had reached US$236.5 billion—equivalent to 40 percent of the nation's GDP. Notably, FDI inflows remained a vital component of national investment activity, contributing significantly to gross fixed capital formation in 2023.

The Czech Republic's evolution from a post-communist economy to a market system is also often cited as a success story of economic transformation. The initial success came from privatization efforts in the 1990s. The government sold off state-owned enterprises, particularly in industries such as energy, telecommunications, and transportation, attracting investors from Western Europe and the United States.

The second step was the creation of **CzechInvest** in 1992, an agency focused on promoting the Czech Republic as an attractive destination for foreign capital and supporting the ease of entry for foreign capital.

As in the case of Poland, the Czech Republic's accession to the EU in 2004 marked a turning point speeding up its economic growth. The path to EU membership required the Czech Republic to align its policies with global standards of business and trade. This alignment played a crucial role in stabilizing the country's macroeconomic environment, controlling inflation, and maintaining low unemployment rates. In addition, the government enacted institutional reforms aimed at creating an appealing investment climate, including strengthening property rights, contract enforcement, and modernizing the legal framework to make the country more attractive to both domestic and international investors.

The Czech Republic's FDI-to-GDP ratio grew steadily during this period, supported by large inflows of FDI, particularly in machine tools and automotive parts production, alongside privatization efforts. Foreign direct investment played a particularly significant role in the country's capital formation in the early 2000s, accounting for 27.9 percent of gross fixed capital formation (GFCF) in 2001, 28.7 percent in 2004. Established production facilities in the Czech Republic were a particular attraction for investors, turning it into one of Europe's top automotive hubs, and further boosting its national automotive sector. Škoda, originally founded as a bicycle manufacturer in 1895, became a subsidiary of the Volkswagen Group in 1991, transitioning into one of Europe's leading automobile manufacturers.

The country's strategic location in Europe, coupled with a well-educated and cost-effective workforce, positioned the Czech Republic as a competitive exporter. By 2015, the Czech Republic had solidified its position as one of the strongest economies in Central Europe, and consistently ranked high in global indexes for ease of doing business. As the economy strengthened and labor costs increased, investors gradually shifted their focus toward less labor-intensive areas and concentrated on more high-value sectors, such as information technology and R&D, logistics, fueling its export-led growth. However, the industrial sector continues to hold a substantial 32 percent share of FDI. Top investors included Germany, the Netherlands, and Austria, alongside significant investments from the United States and South Korea, reflecting the country's appeal to a diverse group of investors.

Table 3.2 presents a comparative analysis of FDI structures across three economies, demonstrating regional investment trends and sectoral differences in 2006.

Table 3.3 illustrates shifts in FDI distribution among economic sectors from 2004 to 2014, indicating evolving investment priorities.

Table 3.2 FDI structure in the Czech Republic, Poland, and Slovakia (2006)

Sectors of the Economy	Czech Republic (%)	Poland (%)	Slovakia (%)
1. Industry	32.0	28.2	38.5
2. Financial services	20.2	22.3	23.0
3. Electricity, gas, and water	15.1	3.5	11.3
4. Wholesale and retail trade, transport repair	12.9	11.2	10.8
5. Transportation, storage, and communication	8.4	9.8	10.0
6. Real estate, lease, and entrepreneurship	5.9	2.2	3.4
7. Development and extraction of mineral resources	2.2	0.3	0.7
8. Construction	1.6	4.0	0.6
9. Social security	1.2	2.8	0.6
10. Hotels and restaurants	0.2	1.2	0.5
11. Health care	0.2	4.5	0.4
12. Agriculture	0.0	0.1	0.2

Table 3.3 FDI structure by economic sector (2004–2014)

Sectors of the Economy	Czech Republic (%)	Poland (%)	Slovakia (%)
1. Industry	34.0	30.0	40.0
2. Financial services	21.0	24.5	24.0
3. Electricity, gas, and water	13.5	5.0	12.5
4. Wholesale and retail trade, transport repair	11.0	13.0	11.5
5. IT sector	5.0	7.5	5.5
6. Transportation, storage, and communication	8.0	8.5	10.2
7. Real estate, lease, and entrepreneurship	7.0	3.0	3.6
8. Development and extraction of mineral resources	1.5	0.5	0.8
9. Construction	2.0	3.5	0.7
10. Social security	1.0	2.5	0.6
11. Hotels and restaurants	0.5	1.8	0.5
12. Health care	0.5	4.0	0.4
13. Agriculture	0.0	0.2	0.2

Slovakia is a good example of a small nation transitioning from a post-communist to a market economy. With a population of 5.4 million and its small size, Slovakia has played an outsized role in the region's economy, particularly in terms of its industrial capacity and integration into global markets.

The country embraced structural reforms, privatization, and a pro-market orientation, positioning itself as a favorable destination for FDI. Its accession to the EU in 2004 and adoption of the euro in 2009 were crucial milestones that reinforced its integration into the global economy.

Several factors have contributed to **Slovakia's success: a deliberate effort to attract FDI, a favorable investment environment, and alignment with global standards.**

Slovakia attracted substantial FDI, particularly in automotive manufacturing, with companies such as Volkswagen, Kia, and Jaguar (Land Rover) establishing their presence. The country became one of the largest car producers per capita, which remains a cornerstone of its economy. As of 2022, the stock of FDI stood at 50.5 percent of GDP, highlighting the role of foreign capital in Slovakia's economic growth. FDI has been primarily directed toward low-cost manufacturing and the financial sector, mirroring trends seen in the Czech Republic.

Slovakia's geographic location in Central Europe, combined with a low-cost and skilled labor force, made it highly attractive to foreign investors. The specific benefits also included favorable tax regimes and public support for foreign investments, with grants covering 20 to 50 percent of investment costs, depending on the project. These grants target job creation, infrastructure development, and fostering innovation, particularly in less-developed regions of the country. The adoption of the euro eliminated currency risks, increased investor confidence, and allowed the country to benefit from greater market integration with its European neighbors, particularly in the automotive and manufacturing sectors. Slovakia's evolution is frequently acknowledged, though it has not been without challenges, particularly due to its reliance on the automotive sector.

Summarizing the CEE experience, what strategic lessons can be drawn? These nations embraced an open, liberal approach to attracting foreign capital by aligning their economies with global market practices and fostering strategic partnerships. Through targeted reforms, investment promotion agencies (IPAs), and policies to enhance the ease of doing business, they successfully channeled capital into critical sectors, creating favorable conditions for sustained growth. Rooted in broader economic growth theories, these actions provide a framework for nations seeking to leverage FDI to drive prosperity. The CEE experience illustrates that a proactive, forward-looking approach can elevate living standards and foster global integration.

3.2 Does FDI Work in Any Situation? Unpacking How Foreign Investment Shaped and Integrated Post-Soviet Economies into Global Markets

Foreign Direct Investment FDI has been a key driver of transformation in many transition economies, as demonstrated by the success stories of Poland, the Czech Republic, and Slovakia. Yet, *the critical question remains: Has FDI truly integrated the post-Soviet economies into the global economic community, or did something go wrong?*

From 1995 to the present, the impact of FDI on driving economic growth across the post-Soviet economies has varied considerably, with uneven distribution of FDI inflows. Immediate observations reveal that Russia and Central Asian economies, particularly Kazakhstan and Turkmenistan, heavily relied on natural resources, attracting FDI primarily from investors seeking access to critical resources such as oil, gas, and minerals. Meanwhile, countries in the Western region of the post-soviet Economies, such as Estonia, Latvia, Lithuania, and Ukraine (though the latter not without its unique challenges), embraced full liberalization, attracting more diversified FDI inflows. In contrast, a small group of countries, including Belarus and Uzbekistan, remained more cautious toward foreign capital, limiting their exposure to international investors.

While FDI contributed to GDP growth and output expansion in many countries, its long-term impact on full integration into global markets remains mixed. Although **Russia** experienced substantial FDI inflows during its peak years, particularly in the energy sector, the country has **shifted toward a less democratic governance model and reduced its global connectivity**. This uneven performance raises **critical questions for policy makers: Has FDI truly led to sustainable economic integration, or has it merely generated short-term economic gains** concentrated in specific sectors? By examining the diverse experiences of these countries, we gain deeper insights into both the limitations and the potential of FDI in transitioning economies.

Analyzing FDI patterns and the speed and direction of institutional reforms enables the categorization **of post-Soviet economies** into three distinct groups: **resource-rich nations** that are heavily dependent on natural resources, **reform-oriented countries** that embraced liberalization, and countries that remained **cautious toward foreign capital**. Examining these divergent paths provides valuable strategic insights for policy makers and business leaders aiming to understand FDI across various economic contexts.

1. **Resource-Rich Countries: Russia, Kazakhstan, Azerbaijan, and Turkmenistan**

FDI has played a positive role in shaping the economic landscape of resource-rich countries such as Russia, Kazakhstan, Azerbaijan, and Turkmenistan. These nations attracted significant FDI, particularly in the energy, oil, gas, and mineral resources sectors, where investments fueled economic growth.

Kazakhstan experienced a surge in FDI during the early stages of its oil sector expansion, with the FDI-to-GDP ratio peaking at 14.6 percent in 2000, illustrating the scale of interest in its burgeoning industry. Similarly, **Azerbaijan** and **Turkmenistan** benefited from FDI in their hydrocarbon sectors, providing critical capital to support economic growth. The oil price crash in 2014, though, showed the vulnerability of these countries in terms of their heavy reliance on minerals and oil exports.

Russia, being the largest economy, attracted FDI in oil and gas extraction and export, heavy industries, and infrastructure. Germany and the Netherlands were at the top of the list, followed by the United Kingdom, the United States, and France. Russia did not engage in proactive support of investors, like the CEE countries; instead, it offered tax incentives.

The 2014 oil price crash, followed by Russia's annexation of Crimea and the onset of the Russia–Ukraine war, had a chilling effect on FDI inflows—a stark contrast to just a year prior when FDI in Russia peaked at a 4.6 percent FDI-to-GDP ratio. By 2022, sanctions and geopolitical complexities led to a shift in investor origins, with China, Cyprus, and the UAE emerging as key players. China strengthened its investment in Russia, focusing on energy, natural resources, and infrastructure, while Cyprus and Bermuda linked to Russian entities domiciled abroad, serving as hubs for round-tripped investments. Russia also started to be more proactive following its deliberate shift to an authoritarian regime. To overcome its vulnerability to oil prices, Russia joined OPEC+ in 2016 to coordinate oil production levels and influence global oil prices.

*What is the strategic insight for policy makers
and business leaders?*

FDI's role as a driver of economic growth is evident. However, in the case of resource-rich countries, it does not necessarily translate into economic prosperity or improvements in living standards. These countries often adopt authoritarian regimes, which, while providing stability and control over resources, raise concerns among international investors regarding investment protection and the rule of law. Resource-rich nations believe they can maintain their appeal due to the critical need of multinational corporations to access resources. In some cases, as demonstrated by the annexation of Crimea, they may even assume they can selectively challenge the international rule of law.

2. Reform-Oriented Economies (Ukraine, Georgia, and Armenia) and Estonia

Each of these nations, despite inheriting unique geopolitical challenges and systemic inefficiencies, has crafted its own approach, yet all converge on market reforms as the central strategy for driving FDI and economic transformation.

Since gaining independence from the Soviet Union in 1991, all of these countries have implemented significant market and institutional reforms, transitioning from a Soviet-style planned economy to a market-driven economy.

Ukraine, the Baltic countries, Georgia, and Armenia have pursued aggressive market reforms to attract diverse FDI inflows. **Georgia**, in particular, implemented aggressive anticorruption reforms, improved property rights, reformed its tax code, and drastically simplified its business regulations, which resulted in a rapid improvement in its ease-of-doing-business rankings and FDI inflows. These reforms positioned Georgia as one of the most attractive FDI destinations in the region, reaching a peak FDI-to-GDP ratio of 12.5 percent in 2007. Recognized for its reforms in ease of doing business, Georgia has successfully attracted FDI in infrastructure, real estate, finance, and logistics. Concurrently, the government's aggressive pursuit of infrastructure development, including the construction of new roads, ports, and logistics hubs, reinforced Georgia's position as a gateway between Europe and Asia. However, the Russian invasion of Georgia in 2008 had shaken investor confidence.

Armenia focused on trade liberalization, banking sector reforms, improving its legal and regulatory frameworks, and efforts to modernize the business environment, which helped to attract investment despite ongoing geopolitical challenges.

Ukraine's FDI-to-GDP ratio peaked at 6.3 percent in 2008, with foreign investments primarily directed toward the industrial sector, agriculture, and, more recently, the IT and service industries. FDI in Ukraine's agricultural sector surged following reforms that allowed the privatization of agricultural land, opening the way for large-scale FDI, with foreign investors playing a key role in enhancing agricultural practices and productivity. Russia's annexation of Crimea and the invasion of Eastern Ukraine marked a significant turning point for the region. Despite these challenges, Ukraine's commitment to reforms, particularly in the energy and IT sectors, allowed it to attract new investments amid ongoing geopolitical threats. Ukraine's IT exports grew by over 20 percent annually between 2015 and 2022, highlighting the sector's resilience and growth potential.

For reform-oriented economies, the key to long-term success lies in implementing transparency and reforms that encourage a favorable investment climate. Ukraine and Georgia, despite geopolitical challenges, demonstrate that a commitment to reform can help attract diverse FDI flows and foster economic resilience.

Estonia's economic transformation, while also classified as reform-oriented, stands in **stark contrast** to many of its former Soviet counterparts. **What Can Other Nations Learn from Estonia's Secret to Economic Transformation?**

Estonia has evolved from a newly independent state into one of Europe's most dynamic digital economies. How did a nation of 1.3 million, with limited natural resources and a communist past, succeed in outpacing other economies and turning into a very competitive player on a global stage? What was the specific role of the state in transforming this nation into a highly appealing destination for MNCs and other investors?

One of the most significant drivers of Estonia's success in attracting FDI and driving economic growth has been its early and ambitious adoption of digital technologies. Estonia actively marketed itself as a digital pioneer and innovation hub, supported by a simultaneous, aggressive adoption of technologies.

The government launched e-Estonia, a nationwide digital transformation initiative, which has made Estonia a global leader in e-governance and digital services. The country offers fully digital public services, including digital identity, e-residency, and online business registration, attracting technology and innovation-focused FDI. Estonia introduced the world's first e-residency program, a digital identity system that allows foreign entrepreneurs to establish and run businesses in Estonia without being physically present. This unique program was marketed globally, positioning Estonia as a hub for digital entrepreneurs and businesses seeking a European market entry. Estonia consistently ranked high in the World Bank's Ease of Doing Business Index.

Estonia's favorable tax regimes include taxes on corporate profits only when profit is distributed as dividends, thus allowing companies to reinvest their earnings without facing immediate tax obligations.

Estonia branded itself as a hub for IT and technology innovation, with government action channeled toward high-value sectors, including information and communication technology, fintech, cybersecurity, and green energy. The country's advanced digital infrastructure attracted investors seeking to capitalize on a well-educated workforce. Estonia has also prioritized education, particularly in science, technology, engineering, and mathematics (STEM) fields. This emphasis has created an impressive talent pool with strong technological capabilities, attracting companies such as Ericsson, Fujitsu, Microsoft, Oracle, and Google, among other tech multinationals. Additionally, English proficiency has contributed to attracting FDI in the tech sector, enabling foreign firms to establish operations that serve both local and global markets. These factors eventually gave rise to Estonia-originated tech success stories, including companies like Skype, Bolt, and Wise.

By combining innovative policies with a focus on long-term growth, Estonia offers a blueprint for countries seeking to leverage FDI and technological innovation to drive economic growth. While most post-Soviet nations exhibit mixed results and inconsistent growth, Estonia rapidly embraced a bold, future-oriented strategy.

3. Low-Income and Slower Reforms (Belarus and Uzbekistan)

In contrast, Belarus and Uzbekistan have been slower to implement market reforms, resulting in significantly lower levels of FDI compared to their neighboring nations. In **Belarus**, foreign investment has been concentrated in a few sectors, including manufacturing and services, but overall inflows remain modest due to state controls and a less open investment environment. **Uzbekistan** saw its peak FDI-to-GDP ratio of 2.5 percent in 2008, driven by investments in natural resources and agriculture. The country's internal resources alone have proven insufficient to drive substantial GDP expansion, highlighting the critical need for external capital. Gradual efforts to open Uzbekistan's economy, reduce state control in certain sectors, and improve the business climate have led to a slow but steady increase in FDI flows into sectors beyond natural resources, such as agriculture, manufacturing, and tourism, as shown in Table 3.4.

The important strategic lesson one can draw here suggests that even incremental reforms can unlock new investment opportunities in previously underdeveloped sectors. Countries that diversify FDI beyond natural resources tend to experience higher GDP growth rates and greater resilience.

Table 3.4 offers a selective comparison of countries representing each group: resource-rich, reform-oriented, and slower-reform.

Isolation or Integration? Key Lessons on How Foreign Investment Reshaped Former Soviet States

From 2000 to 2024, FDI has played a varied but transformative role in the economic development of former Soviet states. Resource-rich nations have benefited significantly from investments in the energy sector, but their reliance on a narrow range of industries has limited broader economic and social progress. In contrast, reform-oriented countries that pursued market-driven policies have attracted more diverse FDI inflows, spurring growth in sectors such as infrastructure, manufacturing, and services.

FDI's role as a catalyst for economic growth is clear, yet its effectiveness in fostering long-term global integration is less certain. While reform-oriented countries have diversified their economies and strengthened global ties, resource-dependent nations have missed opportunities

Table 3.4 Selective comparison of FDI inflows: 2014 versus 2023[27]

Country	Year	FDI as % of Gross Fixed Capital Formation	Volume of FDI (US$ billion)	Key source countries	Key sectors
Russia	2014	6.6%	29.15	Germany, Netherlands, Cyprus	Energy, finance, real estate
	2023	1.8%	8.4	China, UAE	Energy, IT, agriculture
Kazakhstan	2014	17.8%	8.5	Netherlands, United States, France	Energy, mining, finance
	2023	6.5%	3.2	Netherlands, United States, Switzerland, Russia	Mining, infrastructure, manufacturing
Ukraine	2014	2.2%	0.41	Germany, Cyprus, United States	Manufacturing, IT, agriculture
	2023	22.8%	4.2	United States, Poland, Germany	IT, agriculture, energy
Georgia	2014	47.7%	1.8	Netherlands, Azerbaijan	Real estate, finance, tourism
	2023	29.1%	1.6	United States, Azerbaijan	Tourism, agriculture, IT
Uzbekistan	2014	4.5%	0.81	Russia, China, South Korea	Energy, agriculture, construction
	2023	8.5%	2.2	China, Russia, South Korea	Infrastructure, energy, manufacturing, agriculture, mining

to broaden their development paths, leaving untapped potential for economic and social advancement. The contrasting trajectories of these countries underscore the critical importance of strategic reforms and diversified investment strategies in leveraging FDI for sustainable growth and integration into the global economy

3.3 China's Dual Engine of Growth: How Did FDI and Domestic Investment Transform Its National Economy?

FDI played a critical role in China's economic transformation and take-off, particularly in the 1990s and early 2000s, by facilitating technology transfer, providing exposure to the latest managerial practices, and forming export-led industrial growth (particularly via Special Economic Zone) and forming industrial bases (particularly in the coastal areas). Special Economic Zones (SEZs) were critical entry points for foreign capital. However, it is important to note that internal direct investment (domestic investment by Chinese entities) has played an equally important and gradually increasing role in driving China's economic growth. Gross fixed capital formation, much of it from domestic sources, has long exceeded $1 trillion annually.

China's remarkable economic rise has been as strategic as it has been transformative. While not considered reform-oriented in the traditional sense, China's evolution from a recipient nation to one of the world's largest FDI investors offers invaluable insights. Few countries have reshaped the global economic order as swiftly and strategically as China. *How did China engineer such growth, and what lessons can other nations draw from its strategy?*

Initial Growth and Expansion—1980s to 1997:

During the 1980s, FDI inflows into China were relatively modest, obstructed by underdeveloped infrastructure, limited experience with multinational corporations, and a lack of familiarity with global business practices. China had not yet integrated into the global economy and lacked the exposure necessary to adopt effective international business strategies. However, the situation began to change with the initiation of economic reforms and the establishment of special economic zones (SEZs), which gave a powerful stimulus for direct investments. The economic reforms initiated in the late 1970s and early 1980s were aimed at transitioning from a centrally planned economy to a market-driven one. The establishment of SEZs allowed foreign investors to operate under more favorable conditions, including tax incentives and lower regulatory barriers, making these zones attractive destinations for investment. The FDI-to-GDP ratio peaked at around 6.0 percent in 1994, driven by large-scale investments in manufacturing, real estate, and infrastructure. By the end of 1996, the accumulated FDI in China had reached US$128 billion. During this initial phase, foreign investments targeted export-oriented sectors, providing critical capital and laying the groundwork for industrial growth. Concurrently, internal direct investments, though smaller in scale, focused on developing infrastructure and basic industries, paving the way for future economic expansion.

Liberalization and Rapid Growth—1997 to 2005:

The period from 1997 to 2005 marked a significant acceleration in FDI inflows, with the volume reaching US$45 billion by 1997. This rapid growth was driven by the liberalization of previously closed sectors and the devaluation of the Chinese yuan between 1992 and 1994, which made Chinese assets more attractive to foreign investors. By 2005, FDI had reached a record US$72.4 billion, solidifying China's position as a major global investment destination.

This phase was characterized by the multifaceted contributions of FDI: It supported capital accumulation while driving industrial modernization through the transfer of advanced technologies and managerial expertise, which are critical for industrial growth. The creation of joint ventures further accelerated the development of modern technologies in China. Technology transfer, which had stalled during the initial stage of reforms, became a prerequisite for foreign capital to enter the country. In the early phases of reform, China's access to advanced technology was limited, but the establishment of joint ventures marked a critical turning point.

Simultaneously, **internal direct investment** continued to expand rapidly, with domestic firms increasingly investing in manufacturing, infrastructure, and real estate. This combined effect of FDI and domestic investment significantly bolstered China's industrial base and overall economic output.

China's strategic approach to FDI has played a pivotal role in the country's economic development, particularly through its

well-structured policies that prioritize sectoral investment. Through policy instruments, China's National Development and Reform Commission (NDRC) guidelines, and the "Catalogue for the Guidance of Foreign Investment Industries" Chinese government steered foreign capital into specific sectors only. Rather than opening its doors indiscriminately, China's **Catalogue for the Guidance of Foreign Investment Industries** classifies industries into four distinct categories: **industries where foreign investment is encouraged, industries where investment is allowed, industries where investment is restricted**, and **industries where FDI is prohibited**. This level of control allowed policymakers to channel foreign capital into high-priority sectors essential to national development, helping China rise on its own terms.

As of 2005, the manufacturing sector remained the dominant recipient of foreign direct investment (FDI) in China, attracting over 60 percent of total inflows. Within this, machinery and equipment manufacturing was a major beneficiary. In contrast, agriculture consistently received a small portion of FDI, estimated at around 1–2 percent.

The financial services sector, previously restricted, began to open more significantly in the early 2000s following China's accession to the World Trade Organization (WTO). It attracted growing foreign interest and received a rising share of FDI by 2005, including investments in banking, insurance, and securities. Prior to WTO accession, foreign banks were permitted to operate in only a limited number of cities and were generally prohibited from offering services in local currency (RMB) to domestic clients.

Approximately 20–25 percent of FDI was directed toward the services sector, encompassing transportation, warehousing, wholesale and retail trade, real estate, education, and research services. This sectoral distribution reflects China's strategic use of FDI to build export-oriented industrial bases while gradually opening and modernizing its services and financial sectors.

The Chinese government's strategic management of FDI inflows has been a critical factor in its economic success, particularly in boosting the manufacturing sector, which has been a cornerstone of China's export-driven growth model. By focusing FDIs on sectors that align with long-term national interests, China effectively utilized FDI to enhance its industrial base, foster technological innovation, and drive economic modernization.

Stabilization (2005–2010) and the Transition to Maturation (2011–2023): Charting China's Economic Path

In 2005, China's FDI inflows were substantial; the peak was influenced by various factors, including the liberalization of the economy and the opening of sectors to FDI. After this, the Chinese government began to reassess its approach to FDI, gradually moving away from relying primarily on tax incentives as a means to attract foreign capital. The Chinese government's decision in 2007 to phase out tax preferences in SEZs signaled a shift toward a more mature approach to the investment environment, where factors like infrastructure, supply chains, and specialized clusters became more important than fiscal incentives. In the decade from 2011 to 2023, China transitioned from an export-driven economy to one focused on domestic consumption and high-tech industries. FDI inflows continued to be strong, but the focus shifted toward technology, services, and R&D and innovation sectors.

By 2023, FDI had become more diversified, with significant investments in technology, services, and renewable energy. The shift from traditional manufacturing to high-tech and service sectors reflects China's broader economic transition toward a more sustainable and innovation-driven growth model. China has consistently increased its investment in R&D, reaching approximately US$458.5 billion in 2023, marking an 8.1 percent year-on-year increase. Internal investments were directed toward high-tech industries, infrastructure, and renewable energy, aligning with China's strategic goal of self-reliance and technological leadership.

Table 3.5 presents details on China's FDI inflows and internal direct investments over key years, illustrating the evolution of investment strategies.

During this phase, while the FDI-to-GDP ratio has declined, the absolute volume of FDI into China has continued to rise, reflecting sustained international interest, especially in high-tech and renewable energy sectors. At the same time, internal direct investments reached unprecedented levels, with the volume of domestic investment far surpassing that of FDI.

Table 3.5 FDI inflows to China and Gross Fixed Capital Formation (2005, 2014, 2023)[28]

Year	FDI as a % of Gross Fixed Capital Formation	Volume of FDI (US$ Billion)	Top donor countries	Top sectors of economy for FDI	Gross Fixed Capital Formation, US$ Billion[29]	Top sectors of economy for internal investments
2005	8.03	72.4	Hong Kong, Japan, United States	Manufacturing, real estate, services	901	Manufacturing, infrastructure, real estate
2014	2.8	128.5	Hong Kong, Singapore, Japan	Manufacturing, technology, services	4,590	Manufacturing, high-tech manufacturing, technology, services
2023	2.2	163.3	Hong Kong, United States, Japan	Technology, renewable energy, services	7,360	Technology, renewable energy, infrastructure

Table 3.6 China's outward FDI (US$ Billion)

US$ Billions	2000	2005	2014	2020	2021	2022	2023
China	0.9	12.3	123.1	153.7	178.8	163.1	147.9

Source: UNCTAD, FDI/MNE database (www.unctad.org/fdistatistics).

Table 3.6 shows trends in China's outward FDI, reflecting the global expansion of Chinese investments.

China's transformation from being a recipient of FDI to becoming one of the world's largest sources of outbound FDI rests on three strategic imperatives: securing strategic resources, acquiring advanced technologies, and expanding global influence.

China's evolution as an FDI donor began in earnest in the early 2000s, as its domestic economy grew rapidly and its enterprises became more competitive globally. Chinese companies, often supported by state-owned enterprises (SOEs) and facilitated by government policies, began investing abroad to secure energy resources, access advanced technologies, and enter new markets. Key sectors for outbound FDI were natural resources, manufacturing, infrastructure, and, more recently, high-tech and financial services. **China's outbound FDI surged particularly after the global financial crisis of 2008, as Chinese firms sought opportunities in distressed markets worldwide.**

By 2023, China's outward FDI had become more diversified, with a significant volume of investments in sectors such as technology, renewable energy, and services. The country's top destinations for FDI included developed economies such as the United States, the United Kingdom, and Australia, as well as emerging markets in Asia, Africa, and Latin America.

Strategic Insights for Policy Makers and Business Leaders

China's approach to managing FDI exemplifies a deliberate, evolutionary strategy, carefully aligning economic objectives with its developmental trajectory. In the early stages of reform, China faced a dual challenge: narrowing the development gap with advanced economies such as Western Europe, Japan, and the United States, while addressing a significant funding shortfall to fuel its growth ambition.

In response, China implemented an open-door policy, strategically inviting foreign capital to bridge gaps in financing, technology, and expertise. This approach enabled China to amass the critical resources necessary for early industrialization, with stringent requirements for technology transfer serving as a cornerstone for foreign investors' market entry. This policy ensured that incoming FDI not only provided capital but also catalyzed technological and managerial upgrades essential for China's economic catch-up.

As China achieved its initial developmental milestones, its strategy evolved. The government began channeling FDI into targeted sectors while fostering a globally competitive talent pool equipped with advanced managerial expertise. **Beyond attracting capital, FDI was leveraged to achieve broader economic objectives: driving productivity and efficiency through the adoption of advanced production methods, climbing the value chain, boosting employment, and strengthening fiscal health through increased tax revenues.**

China also **utilized FDI as a tool for strategic import substitution**, enabling domestic production to replace costly imports and reducing consumer costs. Concurrently, it prioritized building export-oriented industries to assert its influence in global trade. This marked a pivotal shift toward an innovation-driven growth model, positioning China not only as a major recipient of FDI but also as an increasingly significant global investor in its own right.

By seamlessly integrating foreign investment into its broader economic strategy, China turned FDI from a tool of early industrialization into a driver of innovation, competitiveness, and global economic influence.

CHAPTER 4

Designing Investment Strategy

4.1 Strategies of Influence: Core Principles and Macroeconomic Tools for Investment Strategy Design

Leveraging private capital to drive national growth, create jobs, enhance prosperity, and promote economic rebalancing is a key objective of economic strategy. In an era of intensifying global competition for FDI, crafting a strategic, well-balanced approach is increasingly critical.

Yet, persistent misconceptions about FDI often derail even the most ambitious plans. Addressing these challenges is essential to developing a robust investment strategy. Below, we examine the most common misconceptions hindering FDI efforts and present practical strategies to overcome them.

Navigating Misconceptions: Designing a Balanced FDI Strategy

Misconception 1: FDI Flows Are Primarily Determined by the Investment Climate and a Stable Macroeconomic Environment— *FALSE.* While a stable macroeconomic environment—characterized by low inflation, predictable exchange rates, and sound fiscal policies—is essential, it is not sufficient to guarantee substantial FDI inflows. Today's investors increasingly seek regions where these fundamentals are paired with strategic incentives, transparent regulations, and reliable legal frameworks. Attracting and sustaining investment requires a nuanced, multifaceted approach that integrates both macroeconomic stability and microeconomic competitiveness.

Misconception 2: Reevaluating the Focus on MNCs)—*FALSE*. Although MNCs dominate global FDI, their activities may not always align with the strategic ambitions of the host nation, particularly in high-tech and high-growth sectors. In contrast, medium-sized enterprises often bring innovative technologies and niche expertise that align more closely with a nation's domestic strategy and developmental goals.

It is important to challenge the overemphasis on MNCs and the prevailing belief that they are the primary or sole drivers of beneficial FDI. A more nuanced investment strategy should highlight the benefits of diversifying FDI sources to include medium-sized enterprises and niche players, which often bring innovation, flexibility, and alignment with local economic priorities. A balanced approach that fosters partnerships with both MNCs and small-to-medium-sized enterprises (SMEs) can drive sustained, long-term growth.

Misconception 3. Large FDI Inflows Are Possible without Government Regulation—*MOSTLY FALSE*. This may hold true to some extent in countries with well-established institutional market systems. However, it is imperative to develop a transparent system of incentives for foreign investors alongside robust mechanisms for protecting national capital. Clear regulations can only foster a sense of security among investors and ensure that national interests are safeguarded, ultimately making such markets more attractive.

Misconception 4: Expecting Foreign Investors to Show Interest without Government Intervention—*MOSTLY FALSE*. Passive approaches to attracting FDI rarely yield results. Governments must proactively develop a long-term system of incentives that emphasize the host country's strategic advantages while managing and supporting the investment process. This includes creating targeted policies that cater to specific industries and market segments. Such provisions enable the development of customized incentives and strategies that align more closely with sector-specific challenges and opportunities. This approach ensures that investment attraction efforts are not only effective but are also sustainable, driving long-term growth in key areas.

Misconception 5: FDI Leads to Economic Growth Naturally— *MOSTLY FALSE.* While FDI can stimulate economic activity, its benefits are not guaranteed. Effective policy frameworks are essential to ensure that the benefits of FDI will be realized. Without such an incentive to reinvest in the host economy, companies may seek repatriation of capital. While FDI can stimulate local economies, profit repatriation often limits the economic impact on the host economy, reducing its potential for sustained growth and development

A Phased Approach to Attract FDI

To attract a higher volume of investments and drive economic growth, a comprehensive FDI strategy should amplify a country's unique competitive advantages while systematically addressing barriers that divert foreign capital flows. Global best practices in regulating FDI indicate that successful strategies aimed at creating attractive conditions typically encompass three sets of initiatives:

- Enhancement of the investment climate beyond basic essentials;
- Formulation of a specific legal and administrative framework for foreign investors;
- Creation of a system of targeted incentives for FDI.

The investment climate refers to the overall environment in a country that influences the willingness and ability of businesses to invest. It is shaped by factors such as economic policies, legal structures, political stability, and the availability of resources and infrastructure. While improving the investment climate is crucial, it is not sufficient on its own to drive a substantial increase in FDI. As evidenced by the experiences of developing and transition economies, a favorable investment environment must be reinforced by strategic measures, including the establishment of a robust legal framework and the provision of targeted incentives to enhance the country's investment appeal. Studies have demonstrated that the following incentives have proven effective and that nations can significantly improve their prospects by integrating them:

- **Fiscal Incentives:** These range from tax holidays, income tax reductions, and benefits regarding funds for investment and profit reinvestment to accelerated depreciation write-offs, income tax benefits for foreign employees of enterprises with foreign capital, and support for R&D and export.
- **Financial Incentives:** Options include government subsidies to offset FDI initiation costs, preferential loans or loan guarantees, and favorable terms for state-backed insurance. Additionally, direct state co-investment in equity can signal strong support for strategic projects.
- **Other Incentives**, which typically include infrastructure investments, human capital investments, and SEZs.

International bodies such as UNCTAD and the World Bank have criticized incentive practices, warning of a "race to the bottom"—excessively lowering tax rates or offering generous subsidies that erode public revenues and distort global market competition. Despite these concerns, the use of incentives has expanded significantly across both developing and developed economies, with each relying on these measures to enhance investment attractiveness.

Developed economies often focus on financial incentives such as subsidies, preferential loans, and public infrastructure investments, which reduce operational costs and attract foreign firms. In contrast, developing and transition economies prioritize fiscal incentives, mitigating tax burdens to appeal to investors in markets with high entry costs. These tools have become integral to many nations' competitive strategies, underscoring their perceived necessity in securing sustained investment flows.

An effective investment strategy must be built on a coordinated system of organizational measures that align FDI with national development objectives. To achieve this, the following framework outlines a **Strategic Phased Approach** for developing a robust program to attract foreign investment.

1. Identify Priority Investor Segments

↓

2. Identify Sectoral Priorities

↓

3. Identify Preferred FDI Entry Modes

↓

4. Develop an Integrated System of Incentives and Investor Services

↓

5. Launch Coordinated Government Support

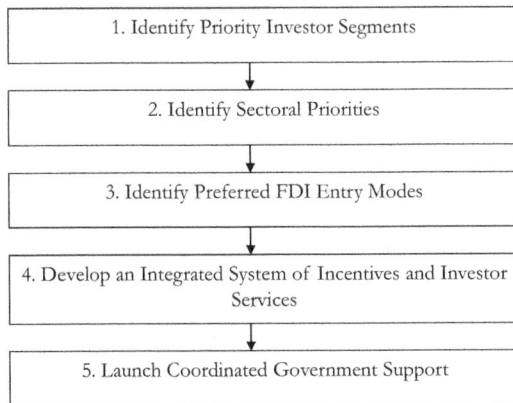

Strategic Phased Approach—Insights and Analysis from Global Best Practices

1. **Identify Priority Investor Segments and Target Foreign Investors from Specific Countries**: Rather than attempting to attract a broad spectrum of investments from across the globe, FDI agencies often narrow their focus to specific countries or regions. This targeted approach focuses on identifying and engaging investors from regions whose strategic priorities align with those of the host region. By focusing on a particular country or set of countries, agencies can tailor their outreach efforts more effectively, increasing the likelihood of securing investment.

2. **Sector-Specific Investment Attraction**: Agencies should strategically target investments for specific sectors of the national economy based on regional strengths and economic priorities. The selection of priority sectors for FDI attraction varies widely, with each national strategy reflecting the country's economic positioning, geopolitical context, unique resources, and overarching national strategic interest.

   Analysis of capital flows has shown that while traditional industries such as textiles and automotive continue to be significant, there is a growing emphasis on advanced manufacturing, high technology, biotechnology, and other knowledge-led industries. Although extractive industries are less of a focus, over 40 percent of regional

FDI agencies still pursue investment in primary sectors. Specialized programs are often developed to attract investors to high-priority sectors such as green technology, biotechnology, health care, and alternative energy, with 75 percent of agencies actively marketing knowledge-intensive industries.

According to the United Nations Conference on Trade and Development (UNCTAD) and the IMF, green FDI initiatives have been on the rise, reflecting a broader global push toward clean energy and sustainable practices. Many countries, including emerging markets, are tailoring their investment policies to attract foreign capital into sectors that promote environmental sustainability, advanced manufacturing, and technology-driven solutions. Additionally, regional FDI strategies often prioritize sectors that align with local economic strengths and resources, further driving the focus on knowledge-intensive and innovative industries.

3. **Type-Specific Investment Targeting**: FDI agencies often align their strategies with the economic development goals of their regions by focusing on particular types of investments. This might involve attracting greenfield investment, encouraging joint ventures, or fostering cooperation with existing investors. According to a UNCTAD survey, 86 percent of regional FDI agencies prioritize deepening relationships with investors already present in the region. The focus tends to be on SMEs rather than large MNCs.[30] Policies that encourage joint ventures are common, especially in developing countries that use them to incentivize foreign investors or to require them to partner with local businesses. This is especially relevant in sectors where there is a strategic need for knowledge transfer and in markets where governments tend to retain some level of control over foreign investments.

4. **Services Provided to Foreign Investors**. The success of attracting foreign investors is closely linked to the quality and breadth of the services provided by FDI agencies. These services range from offering detailed information on the regional business environment to conducting economic feasibility analyses, particularly concerning taxation. The effectiveness of these services is often contingent on the

resources available to the FDI agencies and the involvement of other supporting bodies that can enhance the investor experience.

5. **Tools for Attracting Foreign Investment**. Once the target country, sectoral priorities, and type of investment are identified, agencies deploy a combination of tools and measures to communicate investment opportunities effectively to potential investors. These tools may include marketing campaigns, investment roadshows, and digital platforms that provide potential investors with comprehensive insights into the region's advantages. The goal is to maximize outreach and attract investments that align with regional economic goals.

Integrating Incentives and Investor Services

High-impact investment schemes involving incentives increasingly encompass investor service programs, which, in turn, include government-paid support aimed at boosting profit reinvestment within the host economy. Such initiatives consist of subsidies to support production expansion, investment in sales distribution networks, and human capital investments. However, effective investment promotion goes beyond offering incentives; it requires a well-crafted strategy that actively encourages investment and reinvestment, as well as long-term cooperation.

According to a global survey conducted by the World Bank Group and WAIPA, covering 50 industrialized and developing countries, each dollar invested in professional investment promotion activities can attract up to **US\$189 in foreign direct investment (FDI)**.[31] The most successful strategies target priority sectors and combine precise marketing efforts aimed at specific groups of potential investors and donor countries.

There is a direct correlation between success in attracting FDI and the quality of services provided to investors. High-quality investor services rely on well-prepared, accessible information and timely targeted assistance. High-quality service requires providing complete and factually accurate information about each region and a deep understanding of investor profiles and key factors influencing investment decisions, especially when targeting regional or sector-specific investments

Countries with regional diversity, such as Germany and the United States, significantly enhanced local investment attraction by establishing a network of regional Foreign Investor Promotion Agencies (FIPAs). While this network is often seen in federal states, even centralized economies utilize regional agencies to channel FDI into high-priority regions. These agencies not only promote investment opportunities but also offer targeted pre- and post-investment support to ensure investment retention and investor satisfaction.

Attracting foreign investors requires more than opening up a regional economy; it demands a proactive approach that emphasizes both the host economy's inherent attractiveness and the strategic targeted marketing of its competitive investment advantages to the global investment community. By integrating these incentives with investor services, nations can strengthen their competitive edge. But what are the right tools?

What Macroeconomic Tools Can Turn FDI into a Transformative Driver of Economic Growth?

FDI can be a powerful catalyst for economic transformation, but success depends on how well countries deploy the right macroeconomic tools. From tax incentives to public-private partnerships (PPP), which strategies prove to be the most effective in attracting and sustaining FDI? Can these tools reduce risk and fuel long-term growth? Research indicates that international best practices have led to the establishment of specific norms and standards for state regulation of FDI, as discussed below:

1. **Regulation at Legislative Level:** At this level, state regulation of foreign investment encompasses multiple legal domains: property law with specific provisions on foreign ownership; banking and currency regulations; tax and customs policies; laws governing foreign economic activities; labor and social protection statutes; antitrust regulations; environmental protection policies; and specialized legislation aimed at encouraging or restricting foreign investment both inward and outward flows. Together, these domains form a comprehensive regulatory framework that shapes the investment environment. As discussed in earlier chapters, a stable, transparent regulatory

environment is an essential component of a favorable investment climate.

2. **Regimes of Admission and Operation of Investors:** Procedures for admission (including investment screening and registration) as well as regimes covering investors' operations, national and/or most favored nation treatment, regimes of investors security and protection, compensation in cases of damage, the regulations governing transfers and payments related to investments, mechanisms for dispute resolution, and the structural and policy measures that create a secure environment for investment.

3. **Measures to Stimulate or Restrict Investment:** Targeted incentives are employed to direct FDI toward specific sectors, reflecting national priorities. These incentives may include favorable conditions for participation in privatization, compared to domestic investors, along with a range of tax and customs benefits. Special provisions can further encourage export-oriented production and import substitution while also providing support in addressing labor and social challenges.

    Financial incentives for investors are offered at both national and regional levels, facilitated by relevant government bodies and agencies, and can include grants, subsidies, or partial reimbursements for investments in strategic and critical sectors. Additional incentives to attract specific investment categories include the development of supporting infrastructure (such as transport corridors, utilities, and communications), the establishment of credit and insurance systems for investment projects, and specific measures to encourage reinvestment activity.

4. **Establishing Special Economic, Investment, and Other Zones for Investors:** These zones—encompassing free trade and economic and industrial hubs, among others—provide investors with tailored legal, tax, and customs benefits. Designed to stimulate investment inflows, such zones typically offer incentives for export-oriented production, high-complexity goods manufacturing, and reduced government complexities in relation to operational activities. SEZs are designated areas within a country where business and trade laws differ from the rest of the country, allowing for a controlled and favorable

environment to attract FDI. These defined borders help the government enforce specific regulatory, tax, and customs incentives that apply solely to activities within this zone. A geographical demarcation is essential for administering the unique economic and regulatory conditions that SEZs offer.

5. **Unified Investment Support Systems:** Many countries have adopted a centralized investment support approach, often led by a specialized public or private or hybrid agency (IPA) dedicated to promoting a country as an FDI destination, sourcing foreign investment, and providing guidance and support to investors throughout the entire investment process. Such a unified approach ensures efficient coordination and optimized utilization of resources, contributing to the creation of a favorable investment climate. An attractive investment climate, which includes ease of doing business, is a critical factor for a country's ability to attract FDI and stimulate economic growth.

6. **Coordinated Government Initiatives to Enhance the Nation's Appeal to Global Investors:** A set of measures across all levels aimed at bolstering the country's image, including specific territories designated as attractive destinations for international investors. These efforts include strategic branding, targeted marketing of investment-friendly policies, and highlighting regional advantages to position the nation favorably within the global investment community.

7. **Infrastructure Development.** Infrastructure investment—for example, in transportation, utilities, communication, and networks—improves efficiency in both public and private sectors by lowering operational costs, enhancing connectivity, and facilitating trade. This aligns with the key macroeconomic objectives of increasing aggregate demand and potential output, which, in turn, boosts GDP growth and employment.

In practice, governments use infrastructure spending as part of their fiscal policy tools to stimulate economic activity, especially during economic downturns. For instance, Keynesian theory suggests that infrastructure investments can help counteract recessions by creating jobs and generating demand for goods and services. Endogenous Growth Theory, as discussed in previous chapters, emphasizes infrastructure's role in creating conditions for sustained economic growth, and it is a critical tool for attracting FDI. The EU's Cohesion Policy funds infrastructure projects in less-developed regions, enhancing their attractiveness to foreign investors. China's massive investments in infrastructure, including transportation networks and energy facilities, have been key to attracting FDI, particularly in manufacturing. The United States continues to attract FDI by maintaining world-class infrastructure, particularly in its major economic hubs, such as New York and Silicon Valley.

8. **Investment in Human Capital:** Investment in human capital—such as education, skills training, and health—leads to increased productivity and innovation. By investing in education and upskilling, nations build the essential foundations of intellectual capital that resonate deeply with the needs of high-tech and knowledge-intensive industries, transcending mere financial appeal.

   Economic theories discussed in previous chapters, including Paul Romer's Endogenous Growth Theory, the Solow Growth Model, and the Knowledge–Capital Model, have long supported the notion that human capital creates a self-sustaining cycle of growth, where skilled talent fuels innovation and economic advancement. Keynesian-inspired policies have historically advocated for education, research, and skills development as ways to increase productivity and ensure long-term economic stability.

   As recent FDI flows indicate, global investors are increasingly drawn to regions that prioritize skills development and are renowned for their scientific and technological talent. For example, Estonia's significant investments in promoting science, technology, engineering, and mathematics (STEM) studies and China's efforts to cultivate the next generation of managerial and scientific talent illustrate how nations investing in human capital can enhance competitiveness and sustain growth without relying solely on physical assets. Investing in human capital, including education, upskilling, and health, isn't just an economic strategy—it's a statement of long-term vision.

9. **Fiscal Incentives:** Fiscal incentives are among the most commonly used tools to attract FDI. These instruments include tax holidays, reduced corporate tax rates, and exemptions on import duties. By lowering the cost of doing business, these incentives make it

more attractive for foreign investors to establish operations in a host country. Many EU member-states offer fiscal incentives tailored to specific industries, such as technology and manufacturing, to attract high-value investments. The United States offers a range of tax credits, such as the Research & Experimentation Tax Credit, to incentivize investment in innovation and R&D-heavy industries.

In macroeconomic terms, these incentives support aggregate demand by encouraging businesses to invest, expand operations, and create jobs. Fiscal incentives are considered one factor supporting favorable investment climates, particularly in developing countries.

10. **Trade Policy Instruments** such as tariffs, quotas, and import restrictions. Trade policies, including adjustments to trade barriers, can be used to manage aggregate demand. Reducing tariffs may encourage imports and lower domestic prices, boosting consumer purchasing power and demand. On the other hand, increasing tariffs or restrictions can protect domestic industries and jobs during economic downturns.

In neoclassical and endogenous growth theories, open trade policies—characterized by minimal trade barriers—are typically seen as growth-enhancing because they allow for a more efficient allocation of resources, hence fostering productivity, technological innovation, and competitive markets. Studies cited by organizations like the IMF and World Bank also suggest that lowering trade barriers can stimulate FDI.

A prime example of such beneficial potential is the establishment of the EU's Single Market. Since its inception, the Single Market has eliminated most tariffs and unified regulations among EU member-states, creating a large economic zone that has become one of the world's most attractive destinations for FDI. This unified market provides a common regulatory framework that increases market size, reduces transaction costs, and allows for the free movement of goods, services, capital, and labor, leading to a steady inflow of FDI.

Outside the EU, trade agreements such as the North American Free Trade Agreement (NAFTA) and the United States–Mexico–Canada Agreement (USMCA) have had a similar effect. The reduction of trade barriers between North American economies facilitated the relocation of manufacturing and service facilities, spurred cross-border investments, and bolstered each nation's competitive positioning on the global stage.

Evolving State Roles in Production Investment: Lessons from Global Practices

Governments in both developed and developing economies have increasingly taken active roles in shaping economic and investment processes to balance market efficiency with strategic priorities. This shift is reflected in various measures, such as promoting job creation, developing market infrastructure, and fostering innovation ecosystems. In advanced economies such as the United States and the EU, significant efforts have been made to ensure fair competition by creating favorable conditions for new market entrants. Simultaneously, these governments have implemented investment screening mechanisms to safeguard national security and strategic industries, reflecting a dual approach that promotes open, competitive markets while protecting vital economic interests.

The **European Union** established an EU-wide coordination of FDI screening, which became fully operational in 2020, and has been proactive in leading the harmonization of these screening mechanisms.

Japan presents a distinct case: Its government has been proactive in encouraging foreign investment, particularly in high-priority sectors such as technology, infrastructure, and export-oriented manufacturing. Initiatives such as Japan External Trade Organization's (JETRO) programs have been crucial in facilitating investment through partnerships, innovation ecosystems, and other incentives that promote sectors tied to Japan's economic goals. However, it has also maintained stringent regulations, especially in sectors tied to national security, including technology, energy, and certain manufacturing domains. Japan's Foreign Exchange and Foreign Trade Act (FEFTA) requires preapproval for foreign investments in sensitive areas and the screening of investments in sectors such as defense and cybersecurity.

As discussed above, efforts to attract FDI rely heavily on the strategic use of incentives, which have become an integral part of recipient countries' investment programs. These incentives serve dual objectives: attracting foreign investors while aligning their activities with national economic priorities, such as supporting underdeveloped regions and generating new employment.

Incentives can be direct, such as cash grants and job creation subsidies, or indirect, including tax reductions and exemptions. For large-scale investment projects with the potential to significantly boost local economies, governments tend to allow flexibility and often negotiate tailored agreements directly with investors. This practice is common in developing and emerging economies, aiming to secure high-impact investments that drive regional economic growth through job creation and infrastructure development.

Investment incentives work best when they are part of a holistic strategy that ensures a favorable overall business environment.

In the **Czech Republic**, incentives for both new and existing investors are offered through a specialized national program designed to attract and support investment. These incentives primarily benefit industrial enterprises, technology centers, and entrepreneurship support hubs. Companies in other sectors can also access specific benefits, including job creation incentives, tax breaks for SMEs, grants from local employment centers, tax benefits, and specialized EU funds.

The Czech government has strategically structured these measures to target the early stages of the investment process when financial incentives can yield maximum effect. Incentives are available under certain conditions, however, which they must meet:

- **Infrastructure Development Focus:** Incentives apply to projects involving the acquisition or construction of new facilities as a part of the expansion or modernization of existing production capacities.
- **Investment Thresholds**, depend on enterprise size and whether the project is located in economically underdeveloped regions of the country.
- **Environmental Compliance:** Projects must fully comply with environmental protection standards.

Qualifying new investors may receive corporate tax relief, while existing companies can be eligible for partial exemptions, depending on project parameters and approval by CzechInvest. Additionally, the country offers tailored incentives for projects in technology centers and business support hubs The application for these incentives follows a well-regulated process managed by CzechInvest and associated ministries.

Poland's investment framework reflects a multifaceted, strategic approach to attracting foreign capital. By offering nationwide tax benefits and tailored support for projects that drive innovation and job creation, the country positions itself as a competitive destination for global investors.

Historically, Poland relied on SEZs to offer tax incentives to companies within designated areas. However, in 2018, this model evolved into the Polish Investment Zone (PSI), extending benefits across the entire country. This shift allows companies to access income tax exemptions regardless of location, encouraging broader regional development. Investment projects that focus on job creation, technological advancement, or environmental sustainability are prioritized for state support.

Under the PSI, companies can benefit from corporate income tax (CIT) exemptions and property tax relief, with the possibility of additional grants and subsidies for high-tech and advanced manufacturing initiatives. The scale of these incentives is linked to several factors: size of investment, geographical location (with more favorable terms for economically underdeveloped regions), and how well the investor's project aligns itself with national/host-country economic priorities. Moreover, the Polish government offers comprehensive assistance to ease the process of setting up operations, from navigating regulatory formalities to securing competitive site options.

In **Slovakia,** the government offers a range of investment incentives for projects that contribute to regional development, workforce training, and environmental sustainability. These incentives are targeted at key sectors, including steel production, automotive manufacturing, and synthetic fiber production, as well as projects in R&D, environmental initiatives, and the restructuring of underperforming companies.

China's FDI strategy exemplifies an **evolutionary approach to managing economic openness**. Initially, FDI incentives were introduced as experimental measures within free economic zones. As these trials proved successful, China expanded the practice nationwide, integrating it into broader economic policies.

One of the key instruments of China's FDI strategy has been the establishment of **special investment zones** coupled with **favorable fiscal conditions**. These include SEZs, open cities, technology parks, economic and technological development zones, and free trade zones. Each zone is designed to attract foreign investment by offering **tailored incentives**, such as:

- Reduced corporate income tax rates set at 15 percent, compared to the national average of 25 percent;
- Tax Holidays: Qualified enterprises may receive tax exemptions for a set period, followed by a reduced tax rate;
- Tax rebates on reinvested profits for foreign investors who reinvest profits into encouraged projects may be eligible for tax incentives, such as deferrals or exemptions.

China's strategic use of these zones has facilitated **gradual economic liberalization**, creating a competitive environment for FDI while fostering **regional economic development**. This adaptive approach has made China a global leader in attracting foreign investment.

Synthesizing Key Insights: How Can We Leverage Global Best Practices and Their Analyses to Craft an Effective Strategic Policy for Attracting FDI?

When developing a comprehensive strategy for attracting FDI at the national and regional levels, it is essential to consider the nuanced approaches that can effectively target potential investors. The framework below outlines key considerations for regional and national FDI agencies, focusing on targeted initiatives, tailored services, and impactful communication tools to drive investor interest and engagement.

Four Core Strategies for Enhancing FDI: A Four-Level Approach for Policy Leaders

Level	Strategic Goals and Benefits and the Specific Steps to Be Taken
Level 1: Legislative Framework	Establish a robust legal structure to facilitate FDI. This foundational step involves enacting laws that clearly define investor rights, provide strong legal protections, and set guidelines for foreign investors' access to key sectors. It creates the essential regulatory environment needed to attract and sustain foreign investment.
Level 2: Tax Incentives	Introduce fiscal incentives such as tax holidays, reduced tax rates, and exemptions on reinvested profits. While effective at the early stages of attracting FDI, these measures should be carefully managed. Overreliance on tax breaks can lead to "race-to-the-bottom" scenarios, budgetary shortfalls, and potential misuse by investors. As partnerships deepen, governments should gradually pivot from fiscal incentives to more sustainable support systems.
Level 3: Non-Fiscal Incentives	As the economy matures, transition to higher-order incentives by providing comprehensive government services to foreign investors. Key measures include engineering support, information and consulting services, strategic government support for high-priority projects, upfront public investments in infrastructure, preferential loans, and risk insurance for investors. These services build a more stable, supportive environment, attracting quality investments without the risks associated with extensive fiscal giveaways.
Level 4: Integrated High-Impact Zones	Develop special investment zones that incorporate all previous measures, with a particular emphasis on Level 3 incentives. These zones should prioritize high-tech and innovation-driven sectors, creating clusters that attract cutting-edge industries and drive technological advancement. Integrating fiscal, legal, and non-fiscal supports within these zones encourages sustained growth and long-term investor commitment, fostering economic resilience.

The table presents four essential strategies for boosting FDI, designed for policy makers to optimize investment outcomes and drive sustainable growth.

The study of FDI-related theories and their application across various global contexts highlight the crucial role of governments in shaping economic and investment processes. Over the past several decades, both developed and developing countries have increasingly taken proactive steps to attract and regulate FDI as a means of addressing national economic challenges.

Global experiences in FDI management reveal that effective strategies are built on a balance of legal, fiscal, and strategic supports, each playing an important role in creating a welcoming and competitive environment. **How can these insights be tailored to strengthen your national FDI strategy?**

Strategic Insights for Policymakers to Enhance FDI Flow:

1. **Build on Existing Competitive Advantages**: The first step in designing a successful FDI strategy is to build on the country's unique strengths—whether its natural resources, human capital, or technological infrastructure—and expand beyond those strengths. Identifying these competitive advantages allows for more targeted and strategic positioning in the global investment landscape.

2. **Focus on High-Value Sectors:** What are the key sectors that align with your national growth strategy? How can you create a resilient and sustainable investment ecosystem? Which tools are available? What sectors should be prioritized to maximize growth and sustainability? Focus on sectors that align with national development goals and have the potential for strong growth. Consider which industries can best drive economic expansion, sustainability, and innovation. Prioritizing these sectors will ensure that FDI supports long-term economic goals.

3. **Establish a Robust Legal Foundation:** Ensure clear, transparent regulations that safeguard investor rights and provide consistent guidelines on access to strategic sectors. A solid legal framework fosters confidence and stability, which are critical for long-term investment. Review existing laws and regulations to ensure they are conducive to attracting the right types of investors. This includes ensuring that the regulatory environment aligns well with investor needs without compromising on the desired national outcomes.

4. **Reevaluate the Role of Fiscal Incentives:** What incentives will attract the right investors? While tax incentives can be effective in the initial stages, are they sustainable in the long run? Economies that over-rely on fiscal measures often face fiscal constraints and reduced competitive advantages. Consider a strategic, phased approach to scaling back these incentives as the investment ecosystem matures.

5. **Emphasize Non-fiscal Supports:** Countries that have moved beyond short-term fiscal measures often see greater success. Could infrastructure development, consulting services, and risk mitigation be more effective in building a long-term investment appeal? For example, countries such as Singapore and Germany have used public investment in infrastructure and robust advisory services to make their economies more attractive.

6. **Consider Socioeconomic Impacts**: Weigh the broader socioeconomic benefits of FDI in terms of job creation, technology transfer, health care, and education. How can foreign capital be aligned with national interests? Is there a more holistic approach to developing a resilient and sustainable investment ecosystem that serves dual goals—(1) attracting foreign capital and (2) fostering domestic entrepreneurship?

Leveraging Strategic Insights: How Business Leaders Can Capitalize on FDI Opportunities

Expanding through FDI offers significant opportunities for growth, innovation, and market leadership. However, success requires a strategic approach that aligns with both local and global dynamics. What key strategies can ensure sustainable and profitable international expansion?

1. **Assess the Long-Term Strategic Fit:** Evaluate key factors such as political stability, regulatory environment, infrastructure, and the strength of local industry clusters.

2. **Leverage Local Incentives with a Focus on Value Creation:** Beyond immediate incentives, how well does the target market align with your long-term business objectives? While tax breaks and financial incentives can lower initial costs, is there a clear plan to create sustainable value beyond these benefits? Focus on markets where you can build long-term value through innovation, customer engagement, and local partnerships.

3. **Assess Long-Term Strategic Alignment with the Region:** Evaluate incentives offered by various regions, but look beyond immediate tax benefits to assess long-term strategic alignment and your location

strategy. Consider factors such as infrastructure, regulatory stability, and the local ecosystem's support for innovation. Engaging with SEZs can provide an integrated framework that supports legal, fiscal, and operational needs, positioning your business to be more resilient and adaptive in competitive markets.

4. **Prioritize Strategic Partnerships and Networks:** How can local partnerships amplify your market entry? Collaborating with local firms, government agencies, and industry groups can accelerate market penetration, improve access to resources, and enhance your understanding of the local business environment. Seek alliances that drive growth and add strategic value, rather than purely transactional relationships.

5. **Adapt to the Local Context While Leveraging Your Global Expertise.** It is the role of a business leader to ensure investments contribute meaningfully to economic growth and innovation.

4.2 Designing Tomorrow's Economy: The Case for FDI

Economic science rests on a fundamental principle: Societal needs are unlimited, while available resources are finite. Therefore, a core objective of economic systems is to maximize output through the efficient and effective utilization of all available resources. As societal demands grow alongside populations, the depletion of natural resources and evolving socioeconomic challenges necessitate a focus on sustaining economic growth and power.

Economic growth is defined as the development of a national economy over a specific period, typically measured by increases in GDP, GNP, or national income—either in absolute terms or on a per capita basis. Two primary approaches to assessing economic growth reflect different qualitative aspects: viewing growth through the lens of **total output** emphasizes **a nation's economic power**, while measuring **per capita income growth** focuses on **social well-being** and **living standards**.

In essence, economic growth signifies both quantitative and qualitative improvements in the productivity of production factors, leading to an increase in potential and actual GDP. Economic theory attributes growth to factors influencing both aggregate demand **and** aggregate supply. These include the **quantity and quality of natural resources, human capital, capital stock, and** the **level of technological advancement** embedded within this capital.

Economies evolve through prolonged cycles of expansion and contraction. Known as **Kondratiev waves**, these cycles typically span 40 to 60 years and are associated with transformative shifts in technology and socioeconomic structures. Each new cycle signals a growth phase followed by a recalibration period as economies adapt to innovations. **Today, the global economy stands at a pivotal juncture, shaped by geopolitical realignments, complex socioeconomic transitions, and unprecedented technological advancements**.

In this context, **the Economy of Tomorrow will be defined by the convergence of these trends**, each influencing economic resilience and global societal structures. A strategic imperative for business leaders and policy makers is to be able to visualize **which emerging trends should be**

capitalized on to create a resilient, forward-looking economy. A deep understanding of these cycles, prolonged waves, and emerging trends is essential for strategic positioning and for navigating the evolving context.

By synthesizing the findings from a diverse array of sources—including monographic studies, empirical research, and policy analyses—**the summary that follows provides actionable insights regarding these trends and, more specifically, on positioning FDI strategy as a core driver of long-term resilience and competitive edge**.

Technological Progress: The surge in digital economy investments reflects the growing recognition among MNCs and governments that digital infrastructure and advanced technology are essential for economic resilience, particularly in times of crisis and geopolitical instability. A rapid advancement of AI, blockchain, biotechnology, and network connectivity is set to redefine global business models, with nations and companies prioritizing these areas to maintain a competitive edge. FDI flows are increasingly directed toward tech, science, and innovation hubs to capture emerging STEM talent and foster innovation. Consequently, nations that lead in the development of digital infrastructure and technological innovation are likely to become key destinations for future FDI. Technology drives the frontier of economic growth.

Green Economy Rise: The World Economic Forum's Global Risks Report identifies climate-related risks—such as extreme weather events and inadequate climate adaptation—as some of the most severe economic threats for the coming decade. With projected increases in both frequency and severity, these risks translate into billions in damages each year and increasingly undermine economic and societal stability. In response, governments and businesses are actively forming green public-private partnerships (PPPs) to channel investment into renewable energy, sustainable infrastructure, and climate-adaptive systems.

Investing in green is consistently included in the strategic investment considerations, transforming what was once optional into a core requirement for economic resilience. Such investments aim to mitigate immediate environmental impacts, preempt compounding crises, and address resource shortages, energy dependence, and economic volatility. Greenfield project announcements in GVC–intensive sectors—such as automotive, electronics, and renewable energy—are on the rise. Gen Z and younger generations are also pushing for environmentally responsible investments, adding pressure on companies and governments to accelerate the transition to a low-carbon economy. Green energy, electric vehicles, and climate-resilient infrastructure have moved from the periphery to the core of investment priorities.

Supply Chain Resilience: The global pandemic and recent geopolitical tensions have underscored a critical vulnerability: A supply chain is not only logistical; it is also a strategic asset. Nations that position themselves as reliable supply chain partners are emerging as preferred FDI destinations. In the coming years, MNCs are likely to continue channeling FDI into building logistics hubs, developing transportation corridors, and securing stable access to essential natural resources. FDI increase is anticipated in logistics, network, manufacturing, and infrastructure across Southeast Asia, Eastern Europe, Ukraine, and North Africa.

Socioeconomic Shifts: The future of the global economy isn't shaped solely by technology and infrastructure; it is increasingly influenced by human-centered factors. A growing emphasis on social inclusion, human capital, skills development, and economic and social mobility will define tomorrow's labor market. Nations prioritizing education—particularly STEM education—and inclusive policies will achieve dual benefits: (1) expanding economic opportunities and (2) fostering social stability.

Aligning with Demographic Shifts: As populations age, the demand for age-related products and services will rapidly expand. Strategic FDI can play a critical role by directing resources into sectors such as health care innovation, biotechnology, and gerontechnology or AgeTech, that is, technology aimed at the elderly. By 2050, the "longevity economy" is projected to become a dominant market force, positioning countries that invest in health care and aging-related technologies as global leaders. Investments in traditional health care should not be overlooked, as they remain essential.

Health Care and Smart Infrastructure Opportunities: The need for age-supportive infrastructure (Assistive Technology), particularly in health care and robotics, presents a significant opportunity. Japan's investment in robotics for elderly care exemplifies this approach, addressing domestic needs while creating a scalable model for international markets. The health care sector, particularly pharmaceuticals, has seen increased investment, especially post-pandemic, with rising demand for health care innovation, pharmaceuticals, and aging-related services.

Investment is increasingly directed toward sectors aligned with sustainable development goals, particularly in infrastructure, agrifood systems, health, and education. This includes critical investments in infrastructure spanning across transport, power generation, and distribution, as well as telecommunications and agrifood, spanning agricultural production, processing, fertilizers, pesticides, and R&D. Health and education have seen the most significant growth, reflecting a broader commitment to building resilient, sustainable foundations for future economic growth.

Demographic growth in emerging regions such as Asia, China, Africa, and Latin America is reshaping consumption patterns as the expansion of the middle classes drives demand for quality goods, services, and improved living standards. FDI is expected to follow this upward trend, especially in consumer-driven retail, health care, education, and real estate. Countries with youthful populations and strong consumption growth continue to be attractive markets for FDI. FDI in consumer-focused sectors will be directed toward high-growth economies with demographic dividends. Nations such as India, Indonesia, and select African countries will become essential markets for global companies aiming to tap into rising disposable incomes and expanding consumer bases.

Urbanization and Smart City Development: Today, 57 percent of the world's population lives in urban areas, a figure projected to climb to 64 percent by 2040 and 68 percent by 2050. This steady shift is driving significant transformations in infrastructure demands, sustainability efforts, and resource management needs. These densely populated urban centers generate about 80 percent of the global GDP while presenting rising challenges: Urban areas are responsible for approximately 75 percent of global energy consumption and 60 percent of greenhouse gas emissions. As the global urban population continues to grow, especially across emerging markets, the need for infrastructure modernization and smart city initiatives becomes imminent. From efficient transport systems to digital health care networks, public transportation to waste management, and climate-resilient buildings, tomorrow's cities must be more than densely populated; they must be intelligently designed and have infrastructure that creates a livable environment and ensures sustained quality of life. Regions experiencing the most rapid urban growth, namely Asia and Sub-Saharan Africa, are becoming increasingly strategic destination for FDI aligned with sustainable urban development goals.

Uneven Distribution of Capital: Developed economies contribute to the majority of global FDI outflows, accounting for over two-thirds of total FDI. Corporations from those developed nations are increasingly considering capital allocations to their home markets or in nearby or strategically aligned regions—a recent trend aimed at strengthening supply chain resilience, reducing reliance on distant suppliers, and addressing concerns about geopolitical stability. This shift is especially evident in sectors such as manufacturing, technology, and critical infrastructure, where proximity to key markets has become a strategic priority.

4.3 Beyond Borders: Analyzing the Strategic Flow of Global Investments and Global Power Dynamics

As the global economy enters a new era marked by rapid technological transformation, shifting geopolitical alignments, and environmental imperatives, FDI continues to evolve as **a critical instrument of global economic power and influence.**

In this context, *The Global FDI Landscape* offers a strategic lens for businesses, policy makers, and investors to anticipate future growth trends, identify opportunities, and understand the motivations of leading donor nations. More than a transfer of capital, FDI represents a strategic commitment by MNCs and nations to forge long-term partnerships and shape GVCs. Drawing on insights into emerging trends and the strategic priorities of key donor nations and recipient nations, this analysis examines FDI's potential impact on the "Economy of Tomorrow."

Table 4.1 presents a global snapshot of FDI distribution in 2023, highlighting major recipient countries and sectoral investments.

FDI represents a long-term vision where capital flows are strategically aligned with national priorities and corporate ambitions. From 2010 to 2024, the United States maintained its position as the largest source of FDI, driven by its MNCs' investments in technology, finance, and manufacturing. With more than 100 nations depending on the United States as their primary FDI source, the United States has remained a dominant force in shaping global markets since the last century.

China, the world's second-largest FDI donor, has expanded its influence through initiatives such as the Belt and Road, targeting infrastructure, energy, and telecommunications in developing regions. Meanwhile, Germany leads European FDI, particularly in Central and Eastern Europe, emphasizing high-tech industries and automotive sectors, which have become integral to the region's economic growth.

The United Kingdom and Japan round out the top five FDI sources. The United Kingdom focuses on financial services and technology, while Japan remains a significant investor in technology and automotive sectors. Collectively, these nations showcase the diverse motivations behind FDI, where capital flows signify a blend of economic strategy, resource allocation, and competitive advantage.

Table 4.1 *Global direct investment landscape*

#	Investor countries	Outward direct investment (ODI) destinations	Key sectors for ODI	Top recipients	Source countries for recipients	Key sectors in recipient countries
1	United States	United Kingdom, Canada, Mexico, Brazil, Australia	Finance, insurance, manufacturing, wholesale trade	United States	Japan, Canada, Germany, United Kingdom	Manufacturing, finance and insurance, wholesale trade
2	Japan	United States, Australia, Singapore, China, Germany	Automotive, electronics, technology	China	United States, Singapore, South Korea, Japan, Germany	Manufacturing, pharma, technology services
3	China	United States, Australia, Singapore, Hong-Kong, EU	Manufacturing, IT, infrastructure	Singapore	United States, Japan, China, the UK, Hong-Kong	Financial services, real estate, technology
4	Germany	United States, China, EU countries	Automotive, machinery, chemicals, renewable	Hong-Kong SAR	United States, Japan, China	Financial services, real estate, trade
5	United Kingdom	United States, Netherlands, Germany	Finance, technology, energy, and infrastructure	Brazil	United States, China, Netherlands	Agriculture, energy, manufacturing

Source: Kearney's FDI Confidence Index, unctad.org

Among FDI recipients, the United States, China, Singapore, Hong Kong, and Brazil have drawn substantial foreign investment, reinforcing their roles as global economic hubs. Developing Asia and Oceania have emerged as premier destinations, capturing over 54 percent of global FDI inflows. Led by economies like China and Singapore, the combined region leverages its manufacturing strengths, strategic edge in GVCs, and investor-friendly policies to continue attracting significant capital in sectors defined as priority ones.

While developing economies collectively received US$918 billion in FDI in 2022, a capital shortfall remains. Achieving universal access to infrastructure—such as roads, electricity, water, and sanitation—requires an estimated annual investment of US$1 trillion. Additionally, meeting climate targets demands doubling clean energy investments by 2030, including an extra US$600 billion annually for emerging markets.

Future-Ready Economies: Strategic Investment Imperatives of the World's Leading Nations

Table 4.2 outlines strategic imperatives for direct investments from 2025 to 2035, focusing on long-term investment goals and sectoral priorities.

As the world enters a new development stage, the major economies—such as the United States, China, Japan, and the EU—are recalibrating their strategic imperatives for direct investments. Anchored in their respective national goals, these imperatives reflect each country's unique path to resilience, competitiveness, and technological advancement. From prioritizing energy independence to advancing technological leadership, governments are harnessing both FDI and internal investments to drive long-term strategies. These strategic approaches to FDI demonstrate the varied paths nations are charting to maintain their competitive edge, strengthen influence, and shape the trajectory of the global economy:

- **Global Powerhouses: Technological and Geopolitical Dominance (United States and China)**
- **Sustainable Innovators: Quality of Life and Green Economy (Singapore, Denmark, Netherlands, and Sweden)**
- **Industrial Heritage and Adaptive Innovation (Japan, Germany, South Korea, and France)**

Table 4.2 Projected strategic imperatives for direct investments (2025–2035)

Country	Internal investment sectors	External investment sectors	Top external investment destinations	Strategic imperatives
United States	Technology, renewable energy, infrastructure, defense	Technology, health care, digital economy	Southeast Asia, Europe, Latin America	Technological leadership, energy independence, military superiority
United Kingdom	Technology, green energy, life sciences	Technology, financial services, clean energy	United States, EU, Commonwealth Nations	National resilience, post-Brexit trade relationships, global sustainability
China	Technology, infrastructure, renewable energy	Infrastructure, energy, digital economy	Belt and Road Countries, United States, Germany	Technological self-reliance, global influence, resource security
EU	Green energy, digital transformation, innovation	Sustainable development, digital infrastructure, health care	Africa, Southeast Asia, Eastern Europe	Climate neutrality, digital sovereignty, regional stability
Japan	Technology, automotive, robotics	Technology, manufacturing, digital economy	United States, Southeast Asia, India	Technological innovation, manufacturing leadership, regional partnerships

Group 1: Global Powerhouses—Commanding Technological and Geopolitical Influence (United States and China)

The United States and China are building formidable FDI strategies to consolidate global influence, assert technological dominance, and secure essential resources. Their FDI strategies support critical sectors such as AI, defense, and clean energy, with a particular focus on regions that extend their influence and economic foothold.

Core Imperatives:
- Technological and Military Leadership
- Resource Security
- Strategic Global Influence

The U.S. Approach: The United States uses initiatives such as SelectUSA to attract investments in sectors that include clean energy, infrastructure, and cybersecurity, enhancing economic resilience and technological leadership. Outward FDI focuses on digital infrastructure and development projects in Southeast Asia and Latin America, designed to counterbalance China's Belt and Road Initiative.

China's Approach: China's FDI, with the Belt and Road Initiative at its core, targets infrastructure projects across Asia, Africa, and Europe, securing trade routes and critical resources. Internally, programs such as *Made in China 2025* aim to reduce dependency on foreign technology by driving innovation in robotics, semiconductors, and renewable energy. China's use of state subsidies, tax incentives, and state-backed loans underscores its commitment to becoming a global tech and economic leader.

Group 2: Sustainable Innovators—Quality of Life and the Green Economy (Singapore, Denmark, the Netherlands, and Sweden)

These high-income nations are defined by their commitment to environmental sustainability, high living standards, and global partnerships. Their FDI strategies focus on building green economies, supporting social infrastructure, enhancing digital resilience, and creating models for both quality of life and economic growth.

Strategic Imperatives:
- Environmental Sustainability and Green Economy
- Social Welfare and Innovation
- Global Partnerships for Sustainable Growth

Foundational Priorities:

Domestic Innovation: These countries lead in clean energy, digital infrastructure, and health care, channeling FDI toward transformative green projects. For example, Denmark aims to re-direct global financial flows from fossil fuels to green investments, championing an economic diplomacy that aligns sustainability goals with economic growth. Through strategic partnerships, Denmark fosters global green and digital transformations.

Partnerships: FDI initiatives focus on supporting sustainable projects in developing countries, advancing green technology, smart cities, and social infrastructure to build strong partnerships and elevate living standards globally. Singapore's strategic investments in AI, smart city technology, and digital infrastructure—paired with its business-friendly policies—have secured its position among the world's top five innovators, as highlighted by the Global Innovation Index.

Group 3: Industrial Heritage and Adaptive Innovation—Manufacturing Excellence with Resilience (Japan, Germany, South Korea, and France)

These nations, known for their high-value manufacturing, industrial heritage, and focus on science, are building resilience by advancing traditional industries through technological integration. Focused on sectors such as automotive, robotics, and renewable energy, they drive adaptive, innovation-oriented growth while preserving their industrial heritage.

Strategic Imperatives:
- Industrial and Technological Adaptability
- Cultural Continuity and Economic Stability
- Global Manufacturing Leadership

Japan's Strategy: Japan's 2030 goal of achieving 100 trillion yen (US$652 billion) in FDI underscores its ambition to lead in innovation and economic resilience. Domestically, Japan's Action Plan for Attracting Human and Financial Resources focuses on attracting foreign expertise in green technology, robotics, and digital infrastructure. Meanwhile, Japan continues to assert its presence abroad through strategic investments in infrastructure, renewable energy, and health care across regions such as Southeast Asia and Africa.

Germany's Approach: Germany's Energiewende program channels investment into renewable energy, strengthening its manufacturing core. Inbound FDI flows into high-impact sectors such as energy, health care, digitalization, and the life sciences, reflecting Germany's drive to modernize infrastructure and foster industrial innovation. Outbound FDI supports global supply chains in automotive and green energy sectors, with heavy investments in Europe, Asia, and the Americas to support industrial ecosystems.

Charting the Future: Strategic Insights for Policymakers and Business Leaders

In today's shifting socioeconomic landscape, the role of FDI has evolved from merely attracting capital to actively driving national priorities. Effective FDI strategies now bridge a country's current capabilities and unique strengths with its vision for the future, creating pathways to technological advancement, resilience, and growth. To capture the opportunities of tomorrow's economy, FDI Strategy should be as forward-thinking as it is targeted.

- **Quality over Quantity—Maximize FDI Alignment with National Goals:** Leaders should focus on sectors that align with the country's strategic objectives, ensuring FDI amplifies national goals.
- **Target High-Impact Sectors:** Forward-thinking economies are directing FDI to sectors such as AI, biotechnology, and clean energy. These investments are future-proofing national economies and positioning them for leadership in high-tech and sustainable industries.
- **Balance Openness with Strategic Safeguards:** This delicate balance requires transparent, consistent regulations. It is a strategic dance that involves allowing capital to flow while shielding sectors critical to national integrity. For leaders, it's about finding the "just right" level of openness that allows innovation to thrive within secure boundaries.
- **Reinforce Resilience through Countercyclical Investment:** Directing FDI toward a strategic mix of public infrastructure, health

care, and innovation not only drives output—it builds long-term resilience. Economies that embrace countercyclical investment strategies are better positioned to absorb external shocks, preserve stability, and sustain inclusive economic growth.

For leaders aiming to harness the power of FDI, the roadmap is clear but multifaceted: prioritize quality over quantity, drive resilience through diversification, protect critical resources and industries while fostering openness, and embrace partnerships that multiply impact. By focusing on a green economy, digital transformation, and demographic shifts, today's senior leaders can leverage FDI as a growth mechanism and as an instrument of long-term resilience and influence.

In a world of constant flux, the nations that attract and manage FDI with precision and purpose will be the ones that stand out. For those who get it right, the rewards go beyond prosperity—they secure enduring relevance and a competitive edge. The investments leaders make today are, in every sense, investments in tomorrow's world.

CHAPTER 5

How Strategic Investments Drive Economic Growth: Ukraine's Blueprint for National Prosperity?

5.1 Unlocking Ukraine's Potential: How Strategic Investments Can Position a Nation for Growth

In this chapter, we delve into Ukraine's case as a powerful example of how foreign direct investment (FDI) can act as both a recovery strategy and a cornerstone for national transformation. Ukraine represents an unparalleled case study—its reconstruction requires unprecedented levels of investment following extensive devastation, presenting unique challenges and opportunities for economic revitalization. By applying methodologies outlined in previous chapters, this analysis explores practical approaches to selecting critical sectors that will fuel economic growth and designing mechanisms to attract investment in strategically important areas.

The Ukraine case highlights the necessity of aligning FDI strategies with a nation's specific economic, social, and geopolitical context. This includes strategic importance assessments of key industries, intergovernmental collaboration, and institutional support to create a competitive and resilient economy. More than a recovery plan, Ukraine's model showcases how human development priorities, sustainable infrastructure, and cutting-edge urban design can drive technological innovation and economic diversification.

Crucially, the lessons we can learn from Ukraine transcend its borders. For nations navigating complex phases of transformation—whether due to conflict, economic crises, or structural shifts—Ukraine's FDI-centric approach offers a blueprint for turning adversity into opportunity. The emphasis on channeling investments into sectors that ensure long-term competitiveness, sustainability, and resilience provides actionable insights for other economies seeking inclusive, innovative, and enduring growth.

As we unpack these strategies, this chapter will provide practical tools for examining how one nation's reconstruction journey can inform a universal framework for designing tomorrow's economy.

This section explores the critical role FDI can play in driving economic growth in Ukraine. The analysis focuses on modeling national growth and identifying how a targeted FDI strategy can enhance FDI efficiency and productivity and ultimately serve as a catalyst for Ukraine's sustainable economic development and long-term competitiveness in the global market.

Research Methodology and Sources: This modeling is based on a wide range of sources, including monographic studies; materials from international organizations such as UNCTAD, WTO, IMF, and the World Bank; and legislative acts of Ukraine. The study employs various research methods, including statistical analysis, systematic generalization, and scenario modeling, to assess the impact of FDI on economic growth and to propose mechanisms for stimulating investment in strategically important sectors.

Mapping the Macro Context and FDI

With an ambitious goal to restore GDP to US$300 billion by 2030—exceeding prewar levels—the Ukrainian government aims to establish a foundation for long-term economic resilience. According to UNCTAD, this objective will require US$20 billion in annual investments, while the Ukrainian State Statistics Committee projects a need for US$25 billion to meet broader recovery and infrastructure demands.

The key sectors identified for economic recovery—transportation and energy infrastructure, agriculture, IT, manufacturing, and health care—are central to stabilizing and advancing Ukraine's economy. Investments in infrastructure will reconstruct critical transport and energy systems, reinforcing economic stability, while agriculture remains vital for ensuring food security and sustaining export potential. The IT sector remains crucial for economic resilience, while targeted investments in advanced manufacturing and health care are essential to ensure the economy remains functional and robust amid ongoing conflict. Collectively, these sectors are poised to drive the nation's recovery forward.

The current situation indicates a significant gap between Ukraine's available financial resources and the capital required to achieve its target GDP. In this context, FDI presents several strategic advantages:

1. **Replenishing Limited Domestic Capital:** FDI fills the gap left by insufficient internal savings, providing the crucial capital needed to finance national development.

2. **Facilitating Technology and Knowledge Transfer:** Unlike other forms of investment, FDI drives the exchange of production expertise, advanced management practices, patents, and intellectual capital—assets that can redefine competitive edges.

3. **Expanding Access to Global Markets:** Companies backed by foreign investment often gain easier entry into international markets, creating a path for deep economic integration.

4. **Stability and Predictability over Alternative Investments:** Unlike portfolio investments and international loans, which can be more volatile, FDI offers a stable, long-term commitment that reinforces economic resilience.

Economic growth theories, such as the Solow Growth Model and the endogenous growth theories, posit that higher investment levels (particularly in capital and infrastructure) lead to greater productivity, which can drive economic expansion. Historically, the investment-to-GDP ratio has been used as a key indicator of economic progress, especially in rapidly developing economies.

Higher FDI-to-GDP ratios are linked to economic expansion—a principle supported by many cases and especially evident in Japan, South Korea, and Taiwan. These countries experienced sustained high investment-to-GDP ratios, often exceeding 30 percent, during critical periods of economic development. These high investment levels helped build foundational infrastructure, expand industrial capacity, and enhance productivity, all of which were essential to their economic transformations.

Table 5.1 Ukraine's key macroeconomic indicators
(2008, 2014, 2022)

Year	GDP (US$ billion)	GDP per capita (US$)	Inflation rate (%)	Public debt (% of GDP)	Top 3 sectors receiving FDI
2008	175.81	3,836	22.3	20.0	Finance, manufacturing, real estate
2014	133.51	3,096	24.9	70.3	Finance, agriculture, manufacturing
2022	130.83	3,015	26.6	98.6	Energy, infrastructure, agriculture

Sources: World Bank: GDP, GDP per capita, inflation rates; IMF: Public debt and macroeconomic indicators; National Bank of Ukraine: Inflation and FDI data; UNCTAD: FDI volumes and sectoral distribution. 2022 data include DFI.

Ukraine's economy, strained by ongoing conflict, has experienced fluctuations in GDP, with recent growth exceeding expectations yet remaining below prewar levels. The National Bank of Ukraine (NBU) reports that while economic growth in 2023 outpaced projections, even optimistic forecasts suggest that pre-conflict GDP levels may not be reached until 2030.

Critical infrastructure and production capacities in key sectors—agriculture, manufacturing, and energy—urgently need repair and investment. Reconstruction estimates from the Ukrainian government and the World Bank place Ukraine's funding needs at approximately US$486 billion over the next decade, underscoring the substantial investment required not only to rebuild but also to modernize the economy and bolster global competitiveness.

Domestic resources alone cannot bridge this investment gap. Although internal funding and government spending have driven short-term recovery, addressing the technological lag requires significant investment, which, given the constraints of domestic funding sources, must be sourced from FDI. The domestic credit market is not sufficient to meet structural modernization goals, and a significant share of available credit resources was directed into quick-return sectors, including trade, comprising over 40 percent, leaving high-potential, innovation-driven industries underfunded. FDI, therefore, stands as an essential driver of sustainable growth, offering unique advantages over domestic capital. For Ukraine, this influx could catalyze a leap in production efficiency, particularly in sectors where technological lags have hindered competitiveness.

FDI Quality: Driving Structural Change, Economic Growth, and Resilience

The historical examples of the economies analyzed in previous chapters underscore the importance of directing FDI toward sectors that drive structural change, such as advanced manufacturing, technology, and green energy. These sectors foster GDP growth and contribute to a resilient, diversified economy. However, Ukraine's current FDI structure diverges from these strategic priorities, indicating a need to shift focus toward industries that can build industrial capacity, advance technological capabilities, and integrate into global value chains. This reorientation would maximize FDI's contribution to national development.

The World Economic Forum's *Global Competitiveness Report* highlights FDI in innovation and technology as critical for national competitiveness, supporting Ukraine's alignment with sectors that advance technology and industrial growth. Research from Stanford and Harvard further suggests that FDI in high-tech sectors correlates with stronger GDP growth and heightened global competitiveness. However, these studies also emphasize that the host country's absorptive capacity—its ability to integrate and leverage advanced technologies—is essential for realizing these benefits. For Ukraine, enhancing absorptive capacity would mean investing in education, institutional quality, physical and digital infrastructure, and innovation systems to maximize the impact of quality FDI on long-term economic development. Sectoral focus of Ukraine Investment Strategy will further support optimization of foreign investments for national gains.

Examining national economies through the lens of technological advancement provides critical insights into growth potential, resilience, and competitiveness. Established frameworks, such as UNCTAD's Technological Modes Framework, the OECD's Innovation-Driven Growth Model, and the World Economic Forum's (WEF) Global Competitiveness Index, allow for assessing and prioritizing economic sectors based on their contribution to economic growth. The Technological Modes Framework, in particular, categorizes industries by their technological complexity and potential for economic impact, emphasizing "innovation capacity"—the ability of industries to develop and implement new technologies and processes.

The Technological Modes Framework classifies industries by their technological sophistication, highlighting how different "modes" contribute uniquely to economic growth and innovation. Lower technological modes encompass sectors reliant on basic technologies and natural resources, such as agriculture and mining, which are crucial for economic stability but generally offer limited prospects for rapid growth and innovation. Higher technological modes, in contrast, include sectors such as IT, biotechnology, and advanced manufacturing, characterized by intensive R&D, significant value-add, and the potential to drive economic growth and global competitiveness.

The framework functions as a strategic tool for assessing national strengths and identifying sectors that require targeted investment to advance up the technological ladder. It enables policy makers to prioritize FDI inflows and domestic investments in industries that facilitate technological upgrades and innovation-led growth. By serving as both a diagnostic and guiding tool, the framework empowers users to design a forward-looking, strategic approach for driving national economic growth and transformation.

The framework categorizes industries into different "modes" based on several key metrics, which are used to assess their technological sophistication and economic impact. These metrics include:

1. **Level of R&D Investment**: This metric assesses the proportion of revenue or GDP invested in R&D activities within an industry. Higher R&D intensity typically indicates a higher technological mode.

2. **Innovation Capacity**: This refers to the industry's ability to generate new products, processes, or services, often measured by the number

of patents, technological breakthroughs, and the adoption of advanced technologies.

3. **Value Addition:** This metric evaluates the extent to which an industry contributes to the creation of high-value products or services, typically requiring advanced technology and skilled labor.

4. **Technological Content:** This measures the sophistication of the technologies used in production processes, including the integration of digital tools, automation, and advanced manufacturing techniques.

5. **Global Competitiveness:** Industries are also assessed based on their ability to compete in international markets, which is often correlated with technological advancement.

The Ukrainian economy can be effectively analyzed through the lens of technological modes. Table 5.3 measures technological progress across major sectors in Ukraine, illustrating innovation-driven economic potential.

Ukraine's industrial landscape is diverse, ranging from traditional, resource-based sectors to advanced, innovation-driven industries. The third technological mode includes foundational industries such as thermal power plants, fuel and coal, ferrous metallurgy, and construction

Table 5.2 Technological modes framework

Mode	Key characteristics
Mode 1	Basic resource-based industries with minimal use of technology, primarily focused on raw material extraction
Mode 2	Industries with some mechanization, basic manufacturing processes, and low R&D investment
Mode 3	Sectors utilizing intermediate technologies, with moderate R&D and some automation, including traditional manufacturing
Mode 4	Advanced manufacturing and process industries, significant use of digital technologies, and higher R&D investment
Mode 5	High-tech industries with substantial R&D; innovation-driven, including IT, biotech, and advanced engineering
Mode 6	Cutting-edge sectors with the highest levels of technological innovation, R&D, and global competitiveness, such as nanotechnology and advanced biomedicine

Table 5.3 Technological development index of key sectors in the Ukrainian economy

Sector	Index of technological development	Global ranking	Strategic global importance	Contribution percentage to GDP (2022)
IT and technology	High	Top 30	Yes	5.3
Agriculture	Medium	Top 10	Yes	10.6
Metals and mining	Medium	Top 20	Yes	6.2
Manufacturing	Medium–low	Top 40	Yes	12.0
Energy (renewables)	Medium	Top 35	Yes	4.0
Infrastructure	Low	Top 50	Yes	7.1

materials. While essential for economic stability, these sectors rely on older technologies and offer limited prospects for rapid growth.

The fourth technological mode comprises moderately advanced sectors, including nonferrous metallurgy, chemical and petrochemical industries, and general machine building. These industries have significant production capacity but require modernization to improve their global competitiveness. Industries in the fifth technological mode represent higher technological advancement, covering sectors of electrical engineering, aviation, and pharmaceuticals. These sectors are crucial to drive Ukraine's innovation and its integration into global value chains, and have a great potential for further technological advancement. Advanced machinery and automotive electronics are also sectors with significant R&D and innovation and can be further enhanced through modernization and increased technological adoption.

The sixth technological mode includes Ukraine's most advanced sectors, such as microbiology and medical equipment manufacturing, which are at the forefront of innovation, and hold significant potential for positioning Ukraine as a competitive player in high-tech global markets. These cutting-edge industries, along with emerging sectors such as biotechnology, Information and Communication Technology (ICT), and AI, are crucial for Ukraine's integration into competitive high-tech markets.

This classification not only outlines the current state of Ukraine's industries but also serves as a broader strategic roadmap for targeting investments and policy efforts to elevate technological capabilities and enhance global competitiveness.

Table 5.4 presents a classification of Ukrainian industries by technological mode, highlighting their innovation capacity and modernization prospects.

The analysis of Ukraine's economy through the Technological Modes Framework reveals both the current technological capabilities of various industrial sectors and the strategic importance of aligning FDI with sectors offering the highest potential for innovation and long-term growth. **By examining the qualitative structure of FDI through the lens of technological modes, policy makers and investors can move beyond quantitative assessments to gain a deeper understanding of where investment can most effectively drive technological advancement and economic transformation.** This approach enables the identification of sectoral priorities for foreign investment, ensuring that capital inflows are directed toward industries that will accelerate Ukraine's integration into the global economy.

Analyzing FDI through the lens of technological modes enables a more nuanced understanding of FDI's qualitative impact, moving beyond mere quantitative assessment to identify future sectoral priorities. Research into investment practices in advanced economies highlights that current FDI priorities focus on high-tech industries (fifth and sixth technological modes), a strategy integral to sustaining dynamic growth and global competitiveness.

In contrast, FDI in Ukraine is largely concentrated in low-tech sectors with limited value addition and low technological application, as shown in Table 5.5, which details FDI in Ukrainian industry by technological mode. What is required, therefore, is a strategic shift from the current context.

Analyzing Ukraine's FDI inflows from 2014 to 2022 reveals a predominant focus on low-tech sectors, which has reinforced an industrial structure with limited potential for innovation and long-term competitiveness. Data from the Ukrainian State Statistical Committee, corroborated by the OECD and UNCTAD reports, indicate that a significant portion of FDI was directed toward industries classified under the third and fourth technological modes. These include traditional heavy industries such

Table 5.4 Technological modes of Ukrainian industries

Technological Mode	Sectors of the Ukrainian economy	Global ranking	Key observations
Mode 1	Basic agriculture, raw material extraction (mining of iron ore, coal mining), low-tech traditional manufacturing (e.g., textiles)	Low	Reflects basic, resource-based sectors with minimal technology usage
Mode 2	Primary processing industries (e.g., basic metal processing, cement production), simple construction, low-tech manufacturing	Low	Newly added, includes industries with some mechanization but limited R&D and innovation
Mode 3	Thermal power plants, fuel and coal industries, ferrous metallurgy, basic construction materials (e.g., glass and porcelain)	Medium–low	Industries with established but older technologies
Mode 4	Nonferrous metallurgy, chemical and petrochemical industries, general machine building (excluding advanced electronics), automotive industry	Medium	Sectors requiring modernization to improve technological adoption
Mode 5	Electrical engineering industry, advanced machinery and tool building, pharmaceuticals, advanced chemical processing, automotive electronics, precision instrumentation	Medium–high	Aligned with sectors pushing toward higher innovation, and integration into global value chain
Mode 6	Biotechnology, artificial intelligence (AI), microbiological industry, advanced medical equipment manufacturing, information and communication technology (ICT)	High	Includes cutting-edge sectors with significant R&D and innovation capacity, integral for global competitiveness

Table 5.5 Structure of FDI in the Ukrainian industry by technological modes

Technological Modes	2004 (%)	2005 (%)	2006 (%)	2014 (%)	2022 (%)
Mode 3	46.2	51.6	55.3	50.0	52.0
Mode 4	30.0	27.1	25.4	32.0	28.0
Mode 5	20.8	19.1	18.0	15.0	17.0
Mode 6	3.1	2.2	1.4	3.0	3.0

as metallurgy, construction materials, and energy distribution—sectors characterized by low levels of technological advancement and minimal value addition.

This investment pattern reflects a preference among foreign investors for fast-payback industries with established, low-risk profiles rather than sectors that would catalyze technological modernization or drive the economy toward higher-value industries. Consequently, the focus on these lower-tech sectors has entrenched Ukraine's existing industrial base rather than fostering the development of industries poised for growth. The fifth and sixth technological modes, encompassing sectors such as pharmaceuticals, advanced machinery, and information technology, have seen relatively limited FDI, highlighting a gap between Ukraine's current FDI inflows and the global trend toward prioritizing high-tech investments. This misalignment suggests that while Ukraine remains attractive for its natural resources and traditional industries, there is significant underinvestment in sectors critical for future competitiveness and integration into global value chains. Consequently, Ukraine risks missing the opportunity to reposition itself as a high-tech industrial player. By directing FDI toward sectors with higher technological sophistication, such as advanced manufacturing and renewable energy, Ukraine can begin to close its technological gap with advanced economies.

Redirecting FDI toward high-tech sectors could be pivotal in accelerating Ukraine's economic recovery, transformation, and integration into the global market. This is the right time for strategic shifts in FDI policies to attract investments with a dual focus: (1) supporting immediate economic stability and (2) driving the technological upgrades essential for sustainable growth.

Beyond the above, the geographical concentration of FDI poses additional challenges. The majority of foreign capital is directed toward Ukraine's major urban centers, particularly Kyiv and a couple of regional centers. This concentration restricts the broader economic impact and leaves smaller cities in an as-is state, deepening regional disparities. A more diversified regional FDI strategy, including support for technology hubs and industrial clusters nationwide, would help distribute economic benefits more evenly, fostering balanced growth and regional stability.

Analyzing Ukraine's FDI inflows reveals a concerning trend: **Foreign investors' reinvestment of profits is minimal**. This indicates a preference for repatriating profits rather than reinvesting them into the Ukrainian economy, reflecting a cautious investment approach and investors' hesitancy to commit to the long term.

To address these challenges, Ukraine must craft a strategic framework informed by a deep understanding of investor incentives and a rigorous evaluation of the strengths and weaknesses of its national investment landscape.

5.2 Investment-Driven Growth: A Strategic Model for Ukraine

In Ukraine's evolving economic landscape, the technological caliber of capital investments is a decisive factor in driving growth. Empirical evidence emphasizes that investment activity fuels expansion, while economic theories provide complementary perspectives: Classical frameworks advocate market-driven allocation, whereas Keynesian approaches highlight the strategic role of public investment. Despite their contrasts, both recognize investment as a fundamental engine of economic progress.

To position FDI as a transformative growth lever, Ukraine must optimize the use of scarce capital resources, aligning them with long-term development priorities. Addressing this imperative requires **robust econometric modeling** to reveal the interplay between **investment scale, qualitative composition, and macroeconomic performance.** Such an approach offers **actionable insights for crafting strategies that balance efficiency with sustainable impact.**

The following econometric model captures the dynamics of investment growth[32]:

$$Q_t = a_0 \cdot Q_{t-1} + \Sigma a_i \cdot I_t + Q_0, \qquad (5.1)$$

where a_i represents the model parameters; Q_i is the volume of GDP for the period i; I_t is the volume of investments at time t within the country's economy.

This equation illustrates the relationship between GDP and investments in the previous periods, which serve as catalysts for future economic growth. Applying this econometric model to Ukraine's actual data, V. L. Osetsky derived the following equation of investment growth:

$$Q_t = Q_0 + a_0 \cdot Q_{t-4} + a_1 \cdot I_{t-1} + a_2 \cdot I_{t-2} \qquad (5.2)$$

Lagged investments from the two preceding periods were incorporated to construct a formula for calculating investment growth. The resulting parameter estimates are detailed in Table 5.6.

Table 5.6 Parameters for calculating investment growth

Parameter	Value
Constant level of GDP (Q_0), UAH million	4,883
Autoregression coefficient (a_0)	0.5911
A multiplier for investments with a delay of 3–6 months	1.37
A multiplier for investments with a 6–9 months lag	1.36
Score by the criterion R^2	0.9565

The analysis reveals that approximately 10 percent of GDP (UAH 4,883 million) is generated independently of the broader macro-economic environment and current investment levels. Meanwhile, 59.11 percent of GDP is influenced by the intensity of economic growth in the previous periods, while 30 percent of GDP growth is directly tied to present investment activity. Each UAH invested in the current period yields a return of 1.37 UAH within 6 months and 1.36 UAH within 9 months.

While this econometric model captures the relationship between investment volume and GDP, it overlooks the impact of targeted allocations and technological advancement. The proposed equation below incorporates both investment quantity and quality, providing a more precise representation of investment dynamics in Ukraine's economy, aligning with target growth rates and technical re-equipment of domestic industries. This model offers a holistic approach to understanding how both the quality and quantity of investments drive economic growth and is expressed by the equation:

$$I_{(t+1)} = I_t + \left(\frac{a_t}{N}\right) \cdot I_t + \frac{Q_t \cdot d_{(t+1)}}{K_t}, \tag{5.3}$$

where I_t is the total investment at time t; a_t is the depreciation of fixed assets at time t; N is the standard service life of fixed assets differentiated by industry, Q_t is the GDP at time t; $d_{(t+1)}$ is the projected (or target) GDP growth rate at time t; K_t is the capital efficiency ratio.

A critical factor impacting the capital efficiency ratio is the qualitative structure of investments, in particular their technological efficiency, S_t.

The dynamics of the capital efficiency ratio, K_t, are captured in the following equation:

$$K_{t+1} = K_t + \gamma \cdot K_t \cdot \frac{\Delta S_{t+1}}{S_t} \qquad (5.4)$$

where $\dfrac{\Delta S_{t+1}}{S_t}$ represents a relative change in the weighted average indicator of the technological advancement of investments made; γ represents the percentage change in capital efficiency resulting from a 1 percent increase in technological sophistication.

This dynamic equation illustrates the impact of technological advancements on capital efficiency. By integrating both investment volume and technological quality into the capital efficiency ratio K_t, the equation provides a comprehensive measure of investment quality, reflecting the extent of technological advancement.

GDP capital productivity is calculated as the ratio of GDP over the period under examination to the average capital investment level, using the arithmetic mean of investment at the period's start and end and emphasizing the effectiveness of capital utilization.

This investment growth model allows for estimating the capital investments required to achieve the country's target economic growth rate. A key innovation of this approach lies in its integration of both investment volume and qualitative attributes—particularly technological sophistication—captured by the capital efficiency ratio K_t. The capital efficiency ratio serves as an integrated measure of investment quality, reflecting the degree of technological advancement and capital utilization efficiency. In essence, it represents the qualitative state of capital investments within the Ukrainian economy, indicating both capital productivity, that is, efficiency, and the technological progress embedded in the investments.

Analysis of capital productivity dynamics, expressed in GDP terms, reveals a significant decline in returns on capital, decreasing from UAH 7.91 to UAH 4.76 over the analyzed period. This trend highlights structural weaknesses in the FDI stock, which is heavily concentrated in low-technology sectors and fails to align with the demands of economic recovery and long-term rebuilding. To reverse this trajectory, Ukraine

Table 5.7 Investment growth under the extensive growth scenario

Years	Required investments (UAH million)	Depreciation of fixed assets (%)	Real GDP forecast (UAH million)	Target real GDP growth (%)	Projected return on equity (UAH million)
Year 1	137,076	29.7	575,840.3	7.1	4.39
Year 2	151,115	26.9	619,604.1	7.6	4.30
Year 3	166,858	24.4	669,792.1	8.1	4.21
Year 4	184,602	22.1	727,394.2	8.6	4.14
Year 5	204,664	19.9	793,587.1	9.1	4.08

must adopt a state-level investment strategy that prioritizes attracting FDI to high-technology sectors, fostering innovation, and strengthening the foundation for sustainable growth.

To simulate investment growth scenarios aligned with desired GDP growth targets, the model incorporates key inputs: annual investment volume, fixed asset depreciation, total GDP, real GDP growth rate, and return on capital, sourced from the State Statistics Committee. **This investment growth model provides a robust framework for evaluating various trajectories and their potential economic outcomes, offering actionable insights for policy makers and stakeholders under various scenarios** such as follows:

Scenario 1: Achieving Target Growth Rates: The target GDP growth rate serves as the key indicator. Table 5.7 presents investment modeling results under a scenario that projects an annual increase in real GDP growth by 0.5 percent above the baseline rate, with the FDI structure remaining constant, and GDP growth driven solely by increases in investment volume. Figure 5.1 illustrates projected growth rates for both investments and GDP. If the quality of investments remains unchanged, achieving the target economic growth would necessitate FDI growth outpacing GDP growth, ultimately resulting in reduced capital efficiency. This extensive growth scenario may not represent the most optimal approach

Scenario 2: Targeting Technological Advancement: An alternative target indicator could be the desired level of technological sophistication in investments, which is in line with Ukraine's strategic objectives for

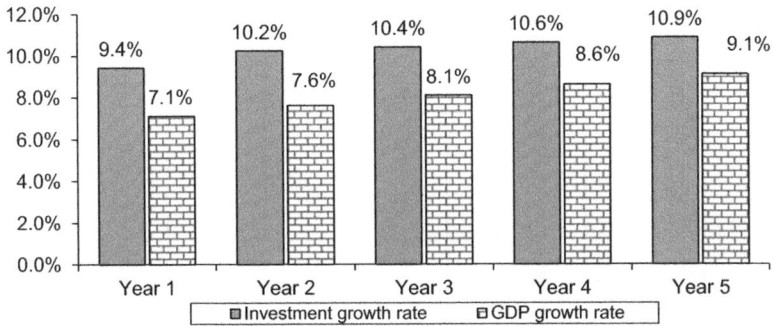

Figure 5.1 Extensive growth scenario

technological development. This scenario proposes economic growth driven by channeling direct investments into higher technological mode sectors. The current technological level of FDI stock corresponds to a mode of 3.65, yielding a capital return of 4.92 UAH on 1 UAH invested.

Targeting a technological mode of 4 and 5 and an additional steady 0.5 percent annual GDP growth rate will be translated into the following results:

Table 5.8 Investment growth under the technological growth scenario

Years	Required investments (UAH million)	Real GDP forecast (UAH million)	Targeted real GDP growth (%)	Projected return on equity (UAH million)	Target average technological advancement of investments (UAH million)
Year 1	137,084	575,840	7.1	5.2	3.8
Year 2	149,654	619,604	7.6	5.4	4.0
Year 3	163,057	669,792	8.1	5.6	4.2
Year 4	177,401	727,394	8.6	5.8	4.3
Year 5	192,814	793,587	9.1	6.1	4.5

Table 5.8 illustrates that optimizing the technological structure of FDI enables economies to achieve targeted growth rates with lower capital requirements, thereby advancing a scenario of innovation-led growth. Initially, investment demand may outpace GDP growth, reflecting an

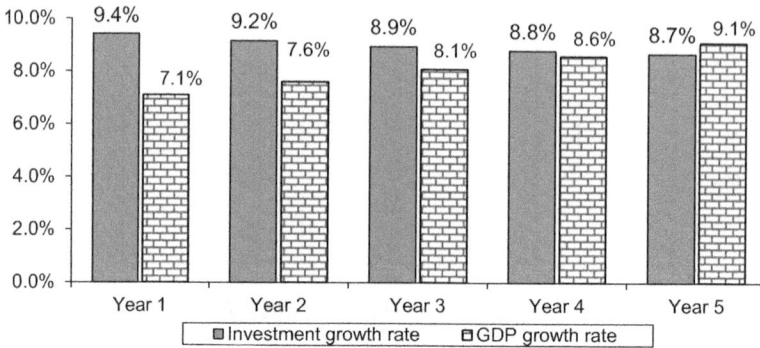

Figure 5.2 *Projected growth rates of investment and GDP, percentage (technological growth scenario)*

extensive phase of development. However, as the technological sophistication of FDI increases, capital efficiency improves. By enhancing productivity and operational performance, such investments lay the foundation for long-term, innovation-driven growth.

The Investment Growth Model allows for the estimation of capital needed to achieve desired levels of economic growth. It is important to recognize that the motivations behind FDI—both in terms of technological composition and volume—often differ from the state's projected requirements for FDI volume and technological mode. This discrepancy necessitates the development of a model that accounts for the dynamics of existing FDI inflows. Based on the assumption that investors make decisions informed by macroeconomic indicators and anticipated profitability, the dynamics of FDI inflows can be represented by the following equation:

$$\Delta I_{(t+1)} = a_0 + a_1 \cdot \Delta BBN_t + a_2 \cdot \Delta R_t \tag{5.5}$$

$\Delta I_{(t+1)}$ is the projected foreign investment growth rate in period $(t+1)$; a_i stands for elasticity coefficients; ΔBBN_t is the real GDP growth rate in the previous period t; ΔR_t is the growth rate of investment return in the previous period t.

The following source data were used (Tables 5.9 and 5.10):

To accurately estimate the dynamics of FDI, it is essential to incorporate a data series with a one-period lag. The parameter estimation results obtained are as follows (Table 5.11).

Table 5.9 *Dynamics of foreign investment returns in Ukraine*

Source data	Year 1	Year 2	Year 3	Year 4	Year 5	Year 6	Year 7
1. Profit of enterprises (UAH million)	9,753.1	13,118.7	10,248.7	13,750.1	33,433.5	48,278.25	52,677.75
2. Share of FDI in disbursed investments (%)	86.90	74.10	78.00	70.60	62.50	92.50	86.30
3. Profit attributable to FDI (UAH million)	8,475.4	9,721.0	7,994.0	9,707.6	20,895.9	44,657.4	45,460.9
4. Volume of FDI (UAH million)	20,537.5	24,143.1	29,001.1	36,010.9	47,044.9	86,140.0	105,930.5
5. Return on foreign investment (p3/p4) (%)	41.3	40.3	27.6	27.0	44.4	51.8	42.9

Table 5.10 *Data series to calculate the dynamics of FDI*

Source data, %	Year 2	Year 3	Year 4	Year 5	Year 6	Year 7
FDI growth rate	17.6	20.1	24.2	33.2	86.7	25.4
Real GDP growth rate	9.2	5.2	9.6	12.1	2.7	7.1
Growth rate of investment return	−2.4	31.5	−2.2	64.8	16.7	17.2

Table 5.11 *FDI parameters*

Estimated parameter	Parameter values
FDI inertia coefficient (a_0)	0.157
Coefficient of elasticity of investment growth rate to GDP growth rate (a_1)	2.203
The coefficient of elasticity of investment growth rate to the growth rate of profitability (a_2)	0.56
Score by the criterion R^2	0.827

The resulting equation is as follows:

$$\Delta I_{(t+1)} = 0.157 + 2.203 \cdot \Delta BBII_t + \Delta R_t \qquad (5.6)$$

Elasticity calculations reveal that the growth rate of FDI is significantly more responsive to changes in real GDP than to anticipated investment returns. A 1 percent increase in GDP correlates with a 2.203 percent rise in FDI, while a 1 percent change in investment returns leads to only a 0.56 percent change in FDI growth. This suggests that foreign investors in Ukraine are primarily strategic, focusing on fundamental economic indicators such as GDP growth and market size, rather than short-term gains. The relatively low sensitivity to investment returns indicates that opportunistic investors—those seeking high short-term returns—constitute a minor share of foreign investment. This stability is advantageous, as national economic growth is rooted in strategic FDI, thereby reducing the risk of substantial FDI volatility and rapid outflows.

Applying the above methodology to analyze FDI dynamics in Ukraine, along with assessing additional investment needs for economic growth and technological advancement, enables forecasting FDI trends under

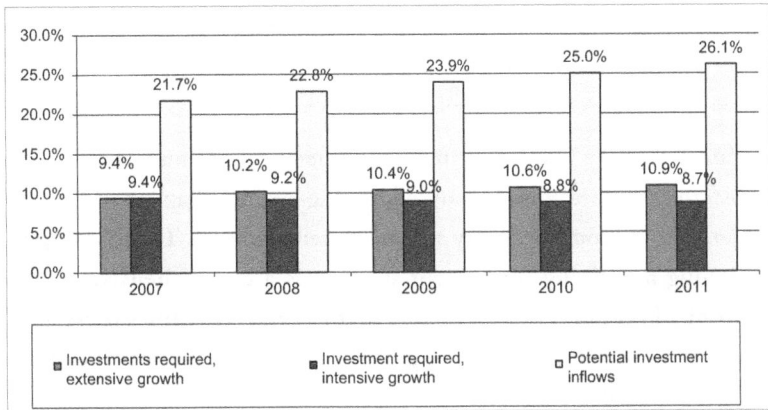

Figure 5.3 Projected growth rates of investment in Ukraine, percentage

various economic growth scenarios (assuming stable FDI profitability—see Figure 5.3).

The study reveals that under each projected economic scenario, FDI could fully cover Ukraine's investment needs for growth and technological progress. Notably, the technological development scenario appears more promising, as it suggests that a smaller volume of high-quality FDI could meet Ukraine's investment requirements sooner, positioning the economy on an accelerated growth trajectory.

This methodology provides a strategic framework for evaluating investment needs across different growth paths and identifying the necessary FDI to fund the preferred development model. To realize these scenarios, Ukraine must ensure a **sufficient volume of FDI**, particularly from foreign sources, as the primary drivers of capital inflow. This requires a **macro-level program focused on stimulating FDI into priority sectors.** A critical first step is an assessment of existing macroeconomic tools governing the investment process to identify regulatory gaps and develop targeted strategies for attracting quality foreign investment.

5.3 Strategic Sectoral Investments: Shaping Competitive Economies in a Rapidly Changing World

Ukraine stands at a defining moment where the promise of FDI as a transformative force depends on addressing systemic gaps that threaten to derail its economic recovery and global reintegration. **The first step in designing a winning investment strategy is a comprehensive assessment of all economic sectors—one that not only identifies these gaps but does so through the lens of global economic evolution and shifting geopolitical dynamics.**

A comprehensive evaluation of Ukraine's FDI stock reveals critical gaps that could impede FDI's potential to become a powerful driver of economic recovery and rebuilding:

- Limited domestic investment to support recovery and subsequent growth and alignment with European and global economic standards;
- Sectoral imbalances in FDI stock that do not align with the nation's long-term strategic interests;
- Mismatched investment objectives that hinder structural adjustments critical for modernization.

This misalignment between Ukraine's strategic economic goals and the actual sectoral composition of FDI underscores the need to prioritize investment in sectors essential for recovery, exponential growth, and enhanced global competitiveness. To address these gaps, **the state should clearly define priority sectors that will drive national economic development and establish targeted incentives to attract FDI in these critical areas.** These **priority sectors should be incentivized to draw substantial capital into Ukraine's real economy**, particularly in industries where the country already demonstrates a competitive advantage and sectors where Ukraine can lead globally.

In parallel, it is essential to enhance the export potential of these targeted industries by increasing the output of high-tech domestic products. This can be achieved through the modernization and re-equipment of production facilities; the application of domestic technologies in processing, storage, packaging, and transportation; and the sale of goods across key sectors such as mechanical engineering, food processing, light industry, and agriculture. Additionally, efforts should focus on solidifying national exporters' positions in established markets while exploring new opportunities abroad. By focusing on these strategic sectors, Ukraine can attract the necessary investment to foster innovation, enhance productivity, and secure a stronger position in the international markets.

A Structured Approach for Setting Sectoral FDI Priorities

Setting sectoral priorities for FDI in Ukraine requires a structured approach aligned with the nation's strategic interests and economic security, as illustrated in the accompanying chart. The first step in establishing these priorities is assessing the strategic importance of individual industries for national economic resilience and high-tech growth. A review of economic literature and original research highlights **three composite indicators that define an industry's strategic relevance to Ukraine's long-term economic goals**.

A Structured Approach for Setting Sectoral FDI Priorities

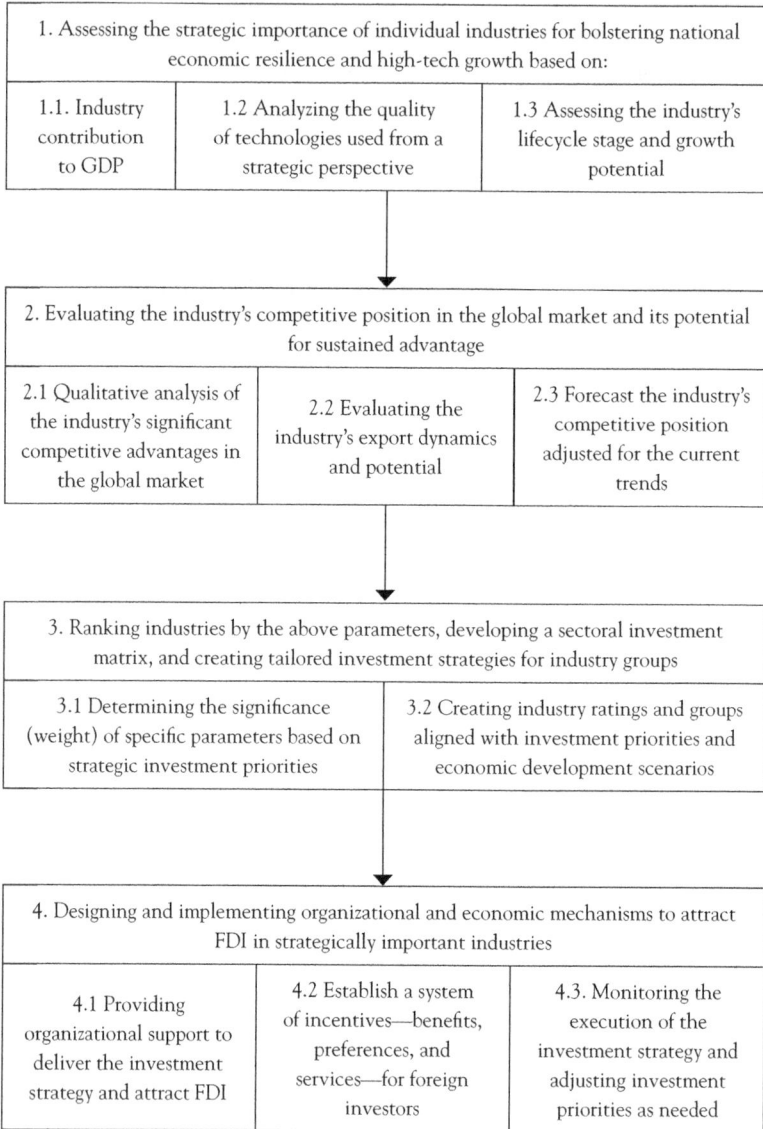

1. Assessing the strategic importance of individual industries for bolstering national economic resilience and high-tech growth based on:		
1.1. Industry contribution to GDP	1.2 Analyzing the quality of technologies used from a strategic perspective	1.3 Assessing the industry's lifecycle stage and growth potential

↓

2. Evaluating the industry's competitive position in the global market and its potential for sustained advantage		
2.1 Qualitative analysis of the industry's significant competitive advantages in the global market	2.2 Evaluating the industry's export dynamics and potential	2.3 Forecast the industry's competitive position adjusted for the current trends

↓

3. Ranking industries by the above parameters, developing a sectoral investment matrix, and creating tailored investment strategies for industry groups	
3.1 Determining the significance (weight) of specific parameters based on strategic investment priorities	3.2 Creating industry ratings and groups aligned with investment priorities and economic development scenarios

↓

4. Designing and implementing organizational and economic mechanisms to attract FDI in strategically important industries		
4.1 Providing organizational support to deliver the investment strategy and attract FDI	4.2 Establish a system of incentives—benefits, preferences, and services—for foreign investors	4.3. Monitoring the execution of the investment strategy and adjusting investment priorities as needed

The first of these core composite indicators is the **level of techno-logical advancement within an industry**, which encompasses the degree to which the industry has adopted advanced scientific and technological innovations, and its role in disseminating these innovations in adjacent or interconnected sectors. This factor is identified as the most critical due to its profound impact on a nation's competitiveness in the global markets. In the context of international competition, industries that actively integrate cutting-edge technologies are better positioned to develop and sustain comparative advantages. Research has shown that technology transformations can contribute up to 80 to 85 percent in determining and solidifying enterprise and industry competitiveness.

Technological advancement serves as the material foundation that determines the technical sophistication of production processes, efficiency of organizational and managerial practices, and overall competitiveness of an enterprise—in terms of cost efficiency, product quality, and speed of innovation, and their subsequent commercialization. In contrast, industries that lag in technological innovation and neglect factors defining global competitiveness will gradually experience deteriorating trade terms and diminished efficiency of foreign trade activities. This creates an additional problem of such industry integration into the global economy.

Global experience from the most successful economic systems demonstrates that high competitiveness and sustained economic growth are correlated with the speed of spread of new technologies and innovation. Economic development and growth are increasingly characterized by the primacy of scientific and technological progress (STP) and the intellectualization of key production factors. Therefore, for Ukraine to enhance its global competitiveness and bolster sustainable economic growth, it is imperative to prioritize and invest in industries that are not only technologically advanced but also play a viral role in the broader dissemination of innovations across the entire economy.

Ukraine should look beyond tactical gains and adopt a long-term perspective, ensuring that the sectoral structure of its economy is balanced across industry lifecycle stages and growth potential. This perspective aligns with the previously discussed Technological Modes Framework, which categorizes industries based on their technological sophistication and innovation potential. By focusing on sectors that fall within the higher technological modes, Ukraine can better leverage FDI to drive economic transformation and secure a more competitive position in the global market. This refined emphasis on technological advancement as a cornerstone of economic strategy provides a clear pathway for Ukraine to align its investment policies with global best practices, ensuring that the country is well-positioned to capitalize on the opportunities presented by rapid technological change.

An analysis of the evolution of scientific, technical, and industrial activities shows that the world is gradually transitioning from the traditional industrial and technological era, which has dominated for much of the twentieth century, toward a new paradigm driven by sustainability and advanced technology. Following the structural crisis of the 1970s, the modern industrial era was characterized by the growth of several key sectors:

1. **Electronics Industry**: Including the production of computers, software, telecommunications equipment, and automation technologies, which have remained central to economic development.
2. **Construction and Resource Extraction**: Focused on critical activities such as the extraction and processing of minerals such as oil, gas, and coal, alongside electricity generation.
3. **Aviation, Space, and Automotive Industries**: These industries, coupled with mechanical engineering, have been pivotal in technological advancements and economic progress.
4. **Intensive Agricultural Production**: Characterized by the application of industrial processes to enhance agricultural productivity.

Recent trends identified by UNCTAD and the World Bank indicate that while these traditional industries continue to play a crucial role, there is an accelerating shift toward sectors emphasizing sustainability, digital transformation, and green technologies. Environmental concerns, driven by climate change and global resource depletion, are leading to a reorientation of industrial priorities. The emerging economic landscape increasingly prioritizes sectors that promote environmental stewardship, renewable energy, and the development of circular economies.

This shift will lead to the formation of new industrial and technological priorities. These priorities are expected to catalyze the emergence of a new socioeconomic paradigm, where sustainability and the protection of human health become central. The future economic system is likely to emphasize integrated, environmentally friendly, and resource-efficient practices, with a strong orientation toward the use of renewable resources. The next 5 years are expected to see significant advancements in technologies and green technologies, including energy efficiency, renewable energy sources, and the digitization of all industries through AI, machine learning, and potentially new methods. These advancements are anticipated to redefine competitive advantages globally, with countries that invest heavily on science positioned to gain economic and strategic benefits.

In this context, innovation will continue to evolve on a new foundation, leveraging robust information networks to integrate scientific knowledge directly into production of goods and services. This transformation will lead to the creation of advanced intellectual and technological complexes, capable of rapid adaptation to changing conditions and demand. As production evolves, the generation of intellectual rent—derived from knowledge and innovation—may become a solid revenue stream for individuals, corporations, and national economies alike.

The structure of global GDP will shift toward a greater emphasis on knowledge- and science-intensive services, particularly those focused on human health protection and longevity, preservation of the nation's gene-pool, sustainable use of resources, protection, and safety. These services are expected to become more profitable and central to economic growth, positioning themselves as key drivers of the future global economy. As this shift unfolds, economies will increasingly adopt an environmental, humanitarian, and innovation-oriented approach, aligning economic growth with the broader societal well-being goals.

The second core integrated indicator is the **strategic importance of sector for ensuring Ukraine's economic stability and security**. While the first criterion focuses on the potential of a sector to position Ukraine favorably in the global market, this indicator emphasizes the role of industries in maintaining the current stability and resilience of the national economy. Even if an industry has a relatively low level of technological advancement, it can still be strategically crucial if it generates a significant share of the country's GDP, employs a large portion of the population, or provides a substantial amount of export earnings. Such industries, due to their immediate economic significance, must be prioritized within the national investment strategy. These sectors require special attention from the government, including the development of tailored investment strategies that ensure their continued contribution to economic stability and growth.

The third factor determining the importance of investment in a given industry is the **competitive advantage and global market competitiveness of the industry**. Sectoral investment priorities should be directed toward industries that possess inherent competitive advantages and can compete effectively on the global stage. By focusing investment in sectors where Ukraine has the potential to lead or excel internationally, the nation can enhance its global economic standing and drive sustainable growth.

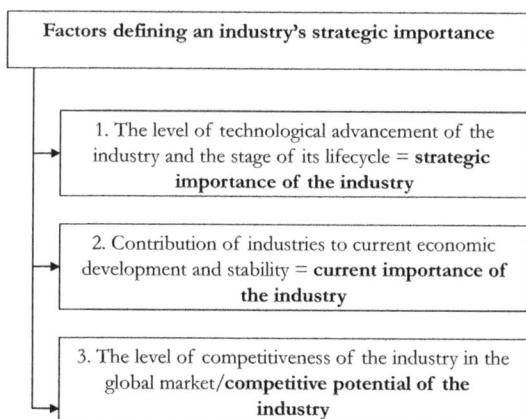

Figure 5.4 Factors defining an industry's strategic importance

Figure 5.4 presents key factor groups that impact the selection of sectoral investment priorities to advance state interests.

The composite indicator for assessing an industry's strategic importance is defined as follows:

$$F = a_1 \cdot T + a_2 \cdot E + a_3 \cdot K \qquad (5.7)$$

Where F is an integral indicator of the industry's investment priority; T, E, K are rank values that reflect the level of technological advancement of the industry (T), its current role in the economy (E), and the level of competitiveness of the industry at the global stage (K); ai are weight parameters of each of the factors of attractiveness of the industries.

Factors Defining an Industry's Strategic Importance

Let's examine each of the three components that collectively define the strategic importance of industries in advancing Ukraine's interests, thereby setting sectoral priorities to drive growth and attract investment.

Factor 1. Sector Technological Advancement

A core element of economic policy is supporting sectors that drive national growth. For an economy like Ukraine, fostering innovation is critical; nations that lag in the global "innovation race" risk marginalization. Ukraine can position itself as an equal international partner only by adopting an innovation-driven development path. Achieving this requires the creation of socioeconomic conditions and incentives that align scientific and technological progress (STP) with the nation's strategic interests and goals.

The technological maturity of an industry closely correlates with its stage in the industry lifecycle, reflecting the sophistication of the technologies it employs. An optimal industrial structure includes the following:

- **Growth Industries:** In the growth phase, industries drive economic expansion through scalability, demonstrating high productivity and creating substantial job opportunities. By leveraging emerging technologies, these sectors broaden their impact, sparking innovation within their domains and across adjacent fields. For Ukraine, they could form the backbone of an economic strategy focused on achieving solid, medium-term growth.
- **Mature Industries:** Maturing sectors operate in established markets with slower growth rates. They primarily drive growth through

efficiency, and process improvements, providing stability and economic security.

- **Emerging Industries**: These sectors, characterized by a high R&D component, have significant potential for rapid scaling, though their current contribution to GDP remains limited. Identifying these sectors is essential for Ukraine's long-term strategic advantage, as they hold the potential to create a competitive edge and shape a resilient economy.
- **Aging Sectors** have established but shrinking markets.

An optimal sectoral split for an innovation-driven growth model would allocate 20 percent to emerging sectors, 35 percent to growth sectors, 35 percent to maturing sectors, and no more than 10 percent to aging sectors—achieving a balance between high-risk innovation, stability, and gradual modernization. This breakdown enables a holistic approach, supporting disruptive innovations while facilitating incremental improvements in established industries, thus fostering sustainable, innovation-driven growth. While emerging and growth sectors serve as the primary engines of economic expansion and job creation, maturing sectors contribute to stability and drive steady, incremental improvements.

An analysis of Ukraine's current economic structure reveals significant sectoral imbalances with respect to industry lifecycles. Over 68 percent of the industrial base is represented by mature and aging industries. Over 46 percent of Ukraine's aging industrial base remains rooted in Soviet-era technologies and practices, contributing to inefficiencies and reduced competitiveness. These enterprises face an urgent need for comprehensive reconstruction and restructuring to restore their economic potential and extend their lifecycles. Growth sectors, vital for medium-term economic development, constitute approximately 26 percent of the economy, while emerging industries—though promising—constitute a modest 5 percent.

A comprehensive overhaul is required to revitalize economic potential and extend industry lifecycles. Investment priorities should be strategically aligned with each sector's technological sophistication, lifecycle stage, and

Table 5.12 Scoring of industries by their technological mode

#	Sectors	Level of technological mode	Rank	Score (from 0 to 1)
1	Aviation and aerospace technologies	6	1	0.097
2	Food industry	3.6	12	0.058
3	Transportation and power engineering	5.2	5	0.084
4	Pharmaceuticals	5.5	2	0.089
5	Ferrous and nonferrous metallurgy	4.1	11	0.067
6	Mechanical and instrumentation engineering	4.7	7	0.076
7	Micro- and radio-electronics	5.4	4	0.088
8	Communications	5.5	3	0.089
9	Chemical industry	4.9	6	0.080
10	Production of high-strength materials	4.6	8	0.075
11	Light industry	3.4	13	0.055
12	Construction	4.3	10	0.070
13	Petrochemical industry	4.4	9	0.071

growth potential. Table 5.12 provides an assessment of Ukrainian economic sectors by technological mode, forming the basis for ranking these industries by investment priority.

Based on a ranked assessment of Ukrainian industries by technological mode, three priority groups emerge, each guiding strategic FDI allocation to maximize economic impact:

- **High Priority**: Industries with the potential to drive Ukraine's future technological breakthrough in the global market, including aviation and aerospace technologies, telecommunications, pharmaceuticals, micro- and radio-electronics, and transport and energy engineering.
- **Medium Priority:** Industries supporting current economic performance, such as chemical and petrochemical sectors, machinery and instrumentation, production of super-strong metals, and construction.

- **Low Priority:** Sectors primarily meeting immediate social and domestic needs, including construction, light, and food industries, with limited strategic significance for Ukraine's long-term innovation goals.

This ranking allows for the formation of a focused FDI strategy, directing investments toward industries with the potential for substantial impact. By prioritizing sectors aligned with higher technological modes, Ukraine can accelerate its economic transformation and solidify its competitive edge globally.

Factor 2. Sector Contribution to GDP

While the focus remains on advancing Ukraine's long-term economic potential, it is essential to balance future-oriented goals with current economic needs. Thus, in evaluating the strategic importance of specific industries, both their role in future growth and their present contributions to economic output—such as GDP, national income, and industrial production—must be considered. These scores will inform the strategic allocation of investments (Table 5.13).

Estimates of individual industries' contributions reveal three distinct groups:

1. **Industries with High Current Importance:** These sectors significantly support Ukraine's economic stability by contributing substantial GDP shares, including ferrous and nonferrous metallurgy, telecommunications, construction, food processing, and petrochemicals.
2. **Industries with Moderate GDP Contribution:** While these sectors make notable contributions, THEY are not leading in GDP impact. Key industries in this category include chemicals, transport and energy engineering, machinery and instrumentation, and light industry.

Table 5.13 Scoring of industries by their contribution to GDP

#	Sectors	Share in GDP (%)	Rank	Score (from 0 to 1)
1	Aviation and aerospace technologies	0.3	13	0.006
2	Food industry	4.7	4	0.102
3	Transportation and power engineering	3.3	6	0.071
4	Pharmaceuticals	1.1	10	0.024
5	Ferrous and nonferrous metallurgy	11.2	1	0.242
6	Mechanical engineering and instrumentation	2.9	8	0.063
7	Micro- and radio-electronics	0.8	11	0.017
8	Communications	6.8	2	0.147
9	Chemical industry	3.2	7	0.069
10	Production of high-strength materials	0.6	12	0.013
11	Light industry	2.1	9	0.045
12	Construction	5.2	3	0.113
13	Petrochemical industry	4.0	5	0.087

Source: State Statistic Committee of Ukraine.

3. **Industries with Minimal Current Contribution**: Sectors that currently have limited impact on GDP and are not strategically critical for Ukraine's immediate economic stability.

Grouping industries by their contribution to current economic development reveals that, at present, low-tech sectors—such as ferrous and nonferrous metallurgy, construction, petrochemicals, and food production—play a primary role in driving economic growth in Ukraine. Telecommunications stand out as the only high-tech industry within this group making a substantial contribution to GDP. In contrast, high-tech industries with strong R&D and innovation potential, including aviation and aerospace, pharmaceuticals, and micro- and radio-electronics, currently occupy a minimal share in Ukraine's production structure. This analysis highlights the need for differentiated investment strategies tailored to each industry group, balancing Ukraine's immediate economic goals with its long-term strategic objectives.

A two-criteria approach to guiding strategic planning and defining investment priorities is presented below.

Two-Criteria Sectoral Matrix

Level of technological sophistication of the industry (strategic perspective)				
	High	Pharmaceuticals, micro- and radio-electronics viation and aerospace technologies	Transportation and power engineering	Telecommunications and communications industry
	Medium	Instrumentation engineering	Chemical industry, mechanical engineering	Construction industry
	Low	Light industry	Petrochemical industry	Ferrous and nonferrous metallurgy, food industry
		Low	Medium	High
	Contribution to economic development (current value of the industry)			

Using a two-criteria sectoral matrix to guide strategic planning, the following sectoral priorities are recommended for tailored investment strategies:

The First Group: Telecommunication, Communication and Network. A tailored investment strategy is essential for this high-priority sector, which is crucial for both future technological growth and its substantial contribution to current economic expansion. This industry should be a top priority for attracting FDI, as these would enable access to advanced technologies, facilitate entry into international markets, strengthen Ukraine's technological competitiveness, and support robust economic growth.

The Second Group: Low-tech industries with medium to high current economic value, including energy, logistics, petrochemicals, food and beverages, machinery and equipment, and agriculture. These sectors are particularly attractive to foreign investors due to factors such as the potential for expanding sales, high profitability, and relatively fast capital returns. Additionally, sectors such as petrochemicals, metallurgy, metal, and mining provide access to critical natural resources, while energy investments are vital for supporting Ukraine's infrastructure resilience.

Given their importance to Ukraine's economic stability and their attractiveness for investors seeking access to transportation routes and essential resources, the development of these sectors should ideally combine FDI with strategies to stimulate national capital investment. This balanced approach will ensure both immediate economic benefits and alignment with Ukraine's long-term strategic interests, particularly in industries essential for securing critical infrastructure and bolstering economic resilience.

The Third Group: High technological mode industries—such as pharmaceuticals, micro- and radio-electronics, aerospace and space, and AI and robotics—are currently playing a limited role in Ukraine's economic output. Regardless of their minimal contribution to national income, these sectors have significant long-term potential to drive Ukraine's economic growth. A phased, mixed investment strategy is recommended to support their development, beginning with domestic investment and gradually introducing FDI as the industries move through the lifecycle.

In the initial stages, the development of high-tech sectors could be supported by the State Budget funds and domestic private investments. This approach signals Ukraine's commitment to high-tech growth, establishing a solid foundation to attract foreign investors seeking strategic partnerships with Ukrainian enterprises.

As these sectors advance, the government should stimulate FDI inflows through incentives such as preferential tax treatment, government-backed investment guarantees, stable public procurement commitments, **and support for international market expansion.** The optimal pathway for attracting foreign capital can encompass establishing joint ventures with international partners, offering multiple benefits:

- **Long-Term Collaboration**: Joint ventures encourage sustained partnerships with foreign investors in high-tech development, enhancing investment stability.
- **Resource Synergy**: By combining Ukraine's scientific and technical resources with the financial and technical capabilities of foreign investors, these partnerships maximize efficiency across R&D, production, and distribution.
- **Reinvestment in Growth**: Joint ventures ensure that a portion of profits remains within Ukraine, enabling reinvestment in the continued expansion of high-tech industries.

A carefully phased approach will bolster Ukraine's technological capacity and establish a resilient framework for sustainable economic growth and innovation.

Factor 3. Export Potential

In establishing final sectoral investment priorities, it is essential to consider not only technological sophistication and GDP contribution but also each industry's global competitiveness. Interconnected global economies and supply chains have transformed the competitive landscape, extending beyond national borders to encompass the global market.

Evaluating sectoral priorities through the lens of global competitiveness is particularly relevant as Ukraine increasingly integrates into global supply chains, capital flows, labor markets, and technology exchanges. **Understanding the competitive position of Ukrainian industries will ensure that investment strategies align with global market realities**.

The current competitiveness of domestic industries is reflected in the structure and dynamics of Ukrainian exports. **By incorporating global competitiveness into investment decisions, Ukraine can more effectively navigate its evolving role in the international economy and optimize its strategic investments.** Table 5.14 **provides statistical data on export growth rates** ranked by competitiveness.

Table 5.14 Industry competitiveness through the lens of export dynamics

#	Sectors	Export growth rate (%)	Rank	Rating (0–1)
1	Aviation and aerospace technologies	66.4	1	0.225
2	Food industry	8.1	11	0.027
3	Transportation and power engineering	41.2	2	0.140
4	Pharmaceuticals	12.7	10	0.043
5	Ferrous and nonferrous metallurgy	34.7	3	0.118
6	Mechanical engineering and instrumentation	7.4	12	0.025
7	Micro- and radio-electronics	17.3	7	0.059
8	Communications	26.2	4	0.089
9	Chemical industry	13.2	9	0.045
10	Production of high-strength materials	22.3	6	0.076
11	Light industry	24.6	5	0.083
12	Construction	15.2	8	0.052
13	Petrochemical industry	5.7	13	0.019

Table 5.15 Sectoral investment priorities—evaluation and scores

#	Sectors	Score—from 0 to 1		
		1. Level of technological advancement	2. Role in current economic development	3. Global competitiveness
1	Aviation and aerospace technologies	0.097	0.006	0.225
2	Food industry	0.058	0.102	0.027
3	Transportation and power engineering	0.084	0.071	0.140
4	Pharmaceuticals	0.089	0.024	0.043
5	Ferrous and nonferrous metallurgy	0.067	0.242	0.118
6	Mechanical engineering and instrumentation	0.076	0.063	0.025
7	Micro- and radio-electronics	0.088	0.017	0.059
8	Communications	0.089	0.147	0.089
9	Chemical industry	0.080	0.069	0.045
10	Production of high-strength materials	0.075	0.013	0.076
11	Light industry	0.055	0.045	0.083
12	Construction	0.070	0.113	0.052
13	Petrochemical industry	0.071	0.087	0.019

Table 5.15 presents a comprehensive evaluation, summarizing the relative importance of investing in each industry. Sectoral priorities are recommended based on the integration of three key parameters: Technological Mode, GDP Contribution, and Global Competitiveness.

To establish integrated estimates for industry priorities in investment and development, it is essential to determine the parameter weightings in the model (5.7). These weightings will guide the prioritization of sectors within the Ukrainian economy and inform sectoral investment strategies. Three distinct development scenarios are considered:

1. **High-Tech Development:** This scenario prioritizes long-term technological advancement and the establishment of a competitive

manufacturing sector, placing secondary emphasis on current development needs.

2. **Competitive Sector Support**: This scenario focuses on strengthening the most competitive sectors that drive current economic growth, with high-tech investments as a secondary priority.

3. **Balanced Development**: Assigns equal weight to technological mode, GDP contribution, and global competitiveness.

Table 5.16 provides the parameter weightings for model (5.7) across these scenarios. Using data from Tables 5.15 and 5.16, formula (5.7) is applied to calculate the priority levels of key sectors in the Ukrainian economy under each scenario. These results illustrate sector distribution according to investment priority (Table 5.17).

International experience demonstrates that without sufficient state regulation, FDI inflows may fail to address sectoral and regional imbalances or align with national priorities. In fact, unregulated FDI can undermine domestic industries and exacerbate disparities. It is worth noting that multinational corporations (MNCs and development finance institutions (DFIs) increasingly consider factors beyond purely economic determinants. A sector-specific strategy allows nations to align FDI with

Table 5.16 Weighting of parameters for investment prioritization across development scenarios

		Development scenarios		
#	Parameters (a_i)	1. High-tech scenario	2. Competitive sectors support scenario	3. Balanced development
1	a_1 (parameter with variable T—level of manufacturability)	0.6	0.15	0.33
2	a_2 (parameter for variable E—role in current economic development)	0.1	0.5	0.33
3	a_3 (parameter with variable K—industry competitiveness)	0.3	0.35	0.33

Table 5.17 Sectoral investment priorities by economic development scenario

Sectoral priorities	Development scenarios		
	1. Development of high-tech industries	2. Development of basic competitive industries	3. Balanced economic development
Industries with a high priority for investment	Aviation and aerospace technologies, transport and energy engineering, ferrous and nonferrous metallurgy, telecommunications and communications	Ferrous and nonferrous metallurgy, telecommunications and communications, transport and energy engineering, aviation and aerospace technologies, and construction	Ferrous and nonferrous metallurgy, telecommunications and communications, transport and energy engineering, aviation and aerospace technologies
Industries with medium priority for investment	Pharmaceuticals, micro- and radio-electronics, chemicals, ultra-light metals, construction industry	Food industry, chemical and petrochemical industry, light industry	Construction industry, chemical industry, food industry, light industry
Industries with low investment priority	Food industry, machinery and instrumentation, light industry, petrochemical industry	Machine and instrumentation, production of ultra-strong materials, micro- and radio-electronics, pharmaceutical industry	Petrochemicals, micro- and radio-electronics, machine and instrumentation, production of ultra-strong materials, pharmaceuticals

national strategic interests and developmental goals, ensuring that FDI inflows reinforce priority sectors.

Common Practices Guiding FDI Regulation

Ukraine's approach to foreign investment should focus on establishing a secure, balanced framework that advances national interests while remaining open to productive foreign partnerships. While forms of access to national sectors for FDI and particular partnership types vary widely, several common practices do nonetheless guide FDI regulation across countries and industries:

1. **Regulatory Frameworks**: Many governments establish legal and regulatory structures that define the extent of foreign participation in specific sectors, often setting limits on foreign ownership, introducing sector-specific rules, or protecting strategic industries.

2. **Sectoral Prioritization**: Countries frequently prioritize certain sectors for FDI based on strategic importance or development goals. High-priority sectors—such as technology, infrastructure, and manufacturing—are often targeted to drive growth, while sensitive sectors like defense and media may face stricter controls.

3. **Incentives and Restrictions**: Attracting FDI to targeted sectors often involves incentives such as tax breaks, subsidies, or preferential policies. Conversely, restrictive measures may limit foreign ownership, require joint ventures with local firms, or entirely prohibit investment in protected sectors.

4. **Sectoral Access Categories**:
   - **Encouraged Sectors**: Industries where FDI is actively promoted, often targeting import substitution or supporting growth in underdeveloped areas.
   - **Unrestricted Investment**: Sectors that welcome foreign capital with minimal restrictions.
   - **Restricted Sectors**: Sectors with foreign ownership limits or regulatory controls in alignment with national interests.
   - **Prohibited Sectors:** Sectors fully restricted to foreign investors, often due to national security concerns or critical industry protection.

5. **Economic Impact Assessment**: Assessing FDI's impact on economic growth, job creation, technology transfer, and overall development goals ensures that foreign investment aligns with national objectives.

These practices help balance the benefits of foreign capital with national interests, ensuring that FDI contributes meaningfully to economic growth while safeguarding strategic sectors. Nations leverage economic tools and administrative controls, such as registration requirements or outright restrictions, to regulate FDI in sectors critical to national security and sovereignty. Commonly restricted areas are as follows:

- **Strategic and Sensitive Sectors**: Industries critical to national security and sovereignty—such as defense, certain extractive industries, transportation infrastructure, agriculture, forestry, media, and financial services—are often shielded from foreign control.
- **Land and Natural Resources**: Limits are often placed on land ownership and the extraction of natural resources to maintain national control over critical resources.
- **Monopolistic Industries**: In sectors with state or public-private monopolies—such as communications, telecommunications, and utilities—foreign investment is often restricted to maintain national oversight over essential services. This approach safeguards strategic industries from foreign dominance where monopolistic control is viewed as essential.
- **Emerging Technologies**: Early-stage advanced technology sectors may limit foreign competition to nurture domestic innovation and shield emerging industries.

Developed nations such as the United States, EU member-states, Canada, Australia, and Germany maintain a balance between welcoming foreign capital and safeguarding national security by implementing sector-specific regulations or overarching legislation. Japan also enforces comprehensive foreign investment laws, and other countries incorporate sector-specific restrictions within a broader legal framework.

Key Strategic Insights

As Ukraine stands at a juncture, the strategic choices it makes in shaping and leveraging FDI will determine not only its path to economic recovery but also its future standing on the global stage. Ukraine's economic resilience hinges on the adoption of integrated strategies that address both immediate crises and long-term growth imperatives. In this context, an innovation-driven growth model is proposed as a cornerstone, emphasizing qualitative advancements in Ukraine's technological investment structure.

This proposed model offers a systematic framework for assessing the volume and technological sophistication required to propel Ukraine's recovery and progress. By prioritizing quality over quantity in FDI, managing enterprise-level challenges, advancing market-oriented management practices, and steering key industries toward sustainable growth, Ukraine can avoid the risks of investment shortfalls that could hinder its reconstruction efforts. Without a substantial shift in the nature and focus of investments, the gap between economic needs and actual growth could widen, undermining recovery momentum.

Despite ongoing geopolitical and economic challenges, Ukraine has benefited from the steadfast support of strategic allies and DFIs. These stakeholders have provided vital capital to sectors including energy, agriculture, technology, and infrastructure—sectors integral to stabilizing the national economy.

By leveraging this capital and strategically realigning FDI toward prioritized sectors, Ukraine is not merely rebuilding; it is establishing a framework for resilience and innovation. Priority sectors such as agriculture, food processing, renewable energy, IT, infrastructure, and advanced manufacturing are identified as critical drivers. Alongside these, strategic industries—including aerospace, power engineering, chemicals, pharmaceuticals, electronics, and advanced defense-related fields such as cybersecurity, AI, lightweight composites, and unmanned systems—hold transformative potential.

These targeted sectors represent not only opportunities for economic recovery but also the foundation for Ukraine's emergence as a global leader in innovation-driven, sustainable growth.

5.4 Ukraine's Resilience Test: Building Investment Appeal amid Wartime Challenges

How Can a Nation Enhance Its Investment Appeal? What are the nation's FDI Attractiveness Factors? Ukraine stands at a critical juncture, grappling with profound challenges and immense stakes in the aftermath of widespread wartime devastation. Russia's systematic war strategy has targeted Ukraine's critical infrastructure—including power networks, water supplies, transportation hubs, and health care facilities—with the explicit aim of crippling economic functionality and public morale. This calculated assault has decimated over 60 percent of Ukraine's power generation capacity, devastated key agricultural and industrial regions, and disrupted global supply chains by destabilizing strategic assets such as the Zaporizhzhia Nuclear Power Plant, grain storage facilities, and the Kakhovka Dam, also leading to severe environmental damage.

The financial scale of recovery is staggering: Estimated as of December 2023, US$486 billion will be required over the next decade to rebuild essential sectors such as housing, transport, energy, and agriculture. Overlaying this physical devastation are deeper systemic vulnerabilities—an elevated debt burden, inflationary pressures, and fiscal deficit—leaving Ukraine's economy precarious and underfunded for the immense ongoing and future tasks. Russia's sustained strategy of regional destabilization seems to persist, further impeding Ukraine's economic outlook.

Attracting FDI under the extraordinary constraints of wartime may appear implausible. Yet, the question remains: Can Ukraine craft a multilayered strategy that not only mitigates immediate risks but also positions the nation for long-term economic modernization and resilience? A strategy centered on stability, infrastructure renewal, and the development of robust economic structures designed to endure and thrive amid geopolitical uncertainty can achieve this goal.

For Ukraine to establish a sustainable FDI attraction framework, it must begin with a comprehensive assessment through **three critical lenses: the macroeconomic environment, sectoral strengths, and the potential of individual enterprises to contribute to national recovery and resilience.**

I. **Macroeconomic Level:** Political stability and regulatory clarity anchor investor confidence, while growth trajectories, inflation trends, and workforce dynamics are scrutinized to gauge operational resilience and competitive edge. Access to essential resources influences production strategies, and tax incentives are evaluated within profitability forecasts.

II. **Sectoral Level:** Sector-specific factors—such as market size, growth potential, competitiveness, technological base, entry and exit barriers, and a strong supply chain—are critical factors shaping investment appeal. Investors are increasingly drawn to sectors that drive growth, offer strategic opportunities, and allow for capitalizing on Ukraine's established strengths and sectoral momentum. By synthesizing macroeconomic trends with sector-specific insights, investors combine immediate opportunities with longer-term evolving market trends.

III. **Enterprise Level:** At the micro level, the attractiveness of individual enterprises is a decisive factor for FDI. This involves evaluating a company's financial position and performance, market position, alignment with broader sectoral and macroeconomic contexts, and strategic fit with investor goals.

I. Macroeconomic Foundations: A Key Driver of FDI Attraction

At its core, a stable and conducive macroeconomic environment is a nonnegotiable prerequisite for attracting FDI. This encompasses political stability, regulatory transparency, a robust legal framework, and sound infrastructure. Ukraine's unique geographic position at the crossroads of European and Asian trade routes, combined with its skilled labor force, scientific potential, and abundant natural resources, reinforces its foundational appeal as an investment destination.

Advanced mathematical and statistical techniques have been employed to calculate the correlation between macroeconomic trends and FDI flows. Through correlation analysis, we quantified the strength and direction of this connection, revealing whether macroeconomic factors directly influence FDI dynamics. These insights provide a data-driven foundation for designing effective and targeted investment strategies.

Statistical analysis reveals a significant correlation between FDI and key macro indicators. Specifically, the data reveal a strong correlation between FDI inflows and the expansion of the domestic market for goods and services. This relationship is cyclical: Robust FDI inflows stimulate growth in trade and services sectors, while the enhanced development of these sectors creates an even more attractive environment for foreign investment. These insights highlight the reciprocal nature of macroeconomic stability and FDI, offering a nuanced roadmap for leveraging economic conditions to sustain and expand a nation's investment appeal (Table 5.18).

Table 5.18 Statistical analysis of the relationship between macro indicators and FDI inflows to Ukraine

Indicators	Correlation
FDI volume—GDP volume	0.96
FDI volume—retail turnover	0.98
The volume of FDI is the volume of the service market	0.94
FDI volume—population income	0.95
FDI volume is the total volume of domestic consumption of goods and services	0.97

While macroeconomic stability forms the essential backdrop for FDI, the true differentiators lie in the specific factors that shape a nation's competitive edge and its unique resources. A detailed analysis of insights from leading global institutions—including JETCO, the Netherlands Foreign Investment Agency, the U.S. Department of Commerce, the EU, and China—provides a nuanced understanding of Ukraine's distinct investment appeal. These factors, ranked by their frequency and prominence across multiple reports, reveal a synthesis of economic, regulatory, and strategic elements that resonate with investor priorities. Together, they provide actionable intelligence for stakeholders aiming to craft Ukraine's investment strategy or gain precise, forward-looking insights into Ukraine's strategic role on the geopolitical map.

1. **Strategic Geopolitical Position:** Ukraine's strategic location at the crossroads of Europe and Asia is consistently emphasized across all reports. This central position provides investors with crucial access to both Eastern and Western markets, enhancing Ukraine's role as a significant trade and logistics hub, including flows of energy and

agricultural commodities. It also presents potential benefits for investors interested in regional distribution. China assesses Ukraine primarily through the lens of its strategic location and market potential. Chinese reports emphasize this potential, describing Ukraine as a vital conduit to European markets and a promising consumer base—critical elements in China's broader geopolitical strategy. Consequently, China is solidifying its influence by investing in critical infrastructure, such as ports, railways, and road networks in Ukraine, seeing Ukraine as both a physical gateway and a strategic anchor in Europe.

2. **Competitive Skilled Workforce Supporting Innovation Ecosystem:** Ukraine's robust network of universities and research institutions drives a rapidly evolving innovation ecosystem, positioning the country as a strategic hub for technology investment. With 80 percent of 19- to 25-year-old Ukrainians enrolled in universities, Ukraine is building a vast pool of tech specialists who draw the attention of major investors. These investors recognize Ukraine's expanding capabilities in critical technology sectors, including IT and engineering, creating a high-value talent pipeline that powers innovation and growth. The European Institute of Innovation and Technology (EIT), part of Horizon Europe—a major EU initiative supporting research and innovation—has established a regional hub in Kyiv to leverage Ukraine's strengths in knowledge creation and diffusion, viewing the city as a strategic center for innovation.

3. **Ukraine's Strategic Role in the Global Raw Materials Ecosystem:** Ukraine's resource endowment positions it as a pivotal player in the global supply of critical raw materials (CRMs), with its reserves of titanium, uranium, and lithium anchoring high-tech, green energy, and defense industries worldwide. As the EU, United States, and other global powers pivot toward decarbonization and technological innovation, Ukraine emerges as a strategic alternative to monopolized supply chains dominated by China and Russia.

Historically, Ukraine has been an important global exporter of minerals, raw materials, and agriproducts for centuries, with substantial reserves and mining capacity positioning the country as a crucial supplier in the global metals market. Raw materials exports were dominated by iron and steel product aggregates: iron and non-alloy steel; iron ore; pig, sponge, and direct reduced iron; and stainless steel, other alloy steel, manganese, and silicon (both as ferroalloys). Both manganese and silicon play critical roles in advanced manufacturing, modern construction, and energy solutions, and they are used in a variety of industries, including battery manufacturing, chemical industry, semiconductors, glass, ceramics, and solar panel production. Ukraine ranks among the top five global suppliers of titanium, a leading producer of kaolin (seventh globally), manganese (seventh), and uranium (ninth). Major destinations of Ukraine exports include Germany, Poland, Turkey, Austria, Italy, and Romania.

As the world started to pivot toward a decarbonized and technology-driven digital economy, Ukraine's raw materials endowment became increasingly critical, positioning the country as an indispensable source of CRMs.

Ukraine stands out as one of the few nations with substantial deposits of titanium ores, beryllium, and uranium—materials critical for high-tech and strategic defense industries, including aerospace, medical, automotive, marine, and nuclear. For example, Ukraine's titanium is indispensable to aerospace and defense, enabling lightweight, corrosion-resistant solutions critical for jet engines and satellites. Its lithium and natural graphite reserves align seamlessly with the EU decarbonization goals, underpinning electric vehicle production and renewable energy systems. Meanwhile, uranium and beryllium reserves bolster global nuclear and advanced military capabilities, creating new avenues for partnerships with the United States, the EU, and beyond.

Ukraine's resource wealth transcends traditional economic value, positioning the nation as a cornerstone for sustainable development, technological innovation, and geopolitical stability. With abundant deposits of critical raw materials—essential for renewable energy systems, electric mobility, and advanced defense technologies—Ukraine enables global transitions to green energy and advanced manufacturing. These resources play a pivotal role in powering sectors such as AI and battery technologies, as highlighted by the U.S. Department of Energy, while aligning seamlessly with the European Union's Green Deal, Raw Materials Strategy, and strategic autonomy objectives. By reducing reliance on monopolized supply chains and bolstering regional security, Ukraine emerges as a critical enabler of Europe's decarbonization and strategic resilience.

This strategic resource endowment, while beneficial, presents significant geopolitical challenges for Ukraine. In 1991, Ukraine declared its strategic vision of aligning with Europe, embracing market mechanisms as the foundation for its economic and cultural evolution. However, this vision is persistently contested by Russia's ambitions to maintain Ukraine within its sphere of influence. These tensions culminated in a full-scale war of aggression, aimed at halting Ukraine's evolutionary development. By seeking control over Ukraine's vast natural resources—including some of the world's most fertile agricultural land (70 percent of arable area, which marks it as the highest percentage in the world)—Russia has attempted to wield leverage over European nations by exacerbating their dependence on critical raw materials and energy.

Bridging Geopolitical Challenges through Reinforced Commitments and Strategic Partnerships

Despite persistent challenges from Russian aggression aimed at leveraging Ukraine's resource base to pressure Europe, Ukraine remains resolute in its reforms. By aligning its governance and regulatory frameworks with EU standards—most notably through its commitments under the Association Agreement and Raw Materials Alliance—Ukraine is signaling its readiness to secure long-term investments and remain a reliable partner in global supply chains.

In tandem with its European integration, Ukraine has embraced transformative reforms, modernizing its extractive industries and adopting sustainability practices to align with EU standards. Initiatives such as the IFC's modernization of the Danube River transport fleets and Ukraine's integration into the European Battery Alliance underscore the collaborative momentum driving these efforts. By diversifying supply chains and creating alternatives to overreliance on China, Ukraine strengthens its appeal as a cornerstone of European resilience and security.

By addressing critical structural pillars—regulatory alignment, judicial independence, anticorruption measures, and property rights protection—Ukraine is signaling its readiness to meet the expectations of a sophisticated global investment community. Central to this effort is the harmonization of legal and regulatory frameworks with EU standards, transparent business practices, and dispute-resolution mechanisms.

This recalibration of economic policies reflects Ukraine's reinforced strategic ambition to become a trusted partner through regulatory excellence and investor protection. It can also pave the way for sustainable, long-term FDI growth that supports its economic transformation.

The EU–Ukraine Partnership: A Win-Win Dynamic

The European Union's engagement with Ukraine underscores support of Ukraine and its strategic vision of aligning with Europe, emphasizing market mechanisms and shared economic and cultural values. For the EU, securing access to Ukraine's CRMs aligns with its goals of decarbonization, industrial innovation, and supply chain resilience. For Ukraine, deeper integration with the EU market translates into modernization, investment, and geopolitical alignment. The modernization of Ukraine's extractive industries, underpinned by improved legal and administrative frameworks, sets the stage for a two-way partnership.

Ukraine's integration into the EU's Raw Materials Alliance and the strategic partnership for CRMs can turn the nation into a solid partner, securing resilient supply chains. Additionally, Ukraine's uranium reserves underpin global nuclear energy and defense strategies, serving as a counterbalance to reliance on Russian and Kazakh suppliers. Beryllium, a key material in advanced military technologies such as jet fighters and satellites, highlights Ukraine's potential role in defense technology supply chains, particularly for the EU and the United States. Meanwhile, graphite, critical for battery and renewable energy technologies, positions Ukraine as a strategic supplier for both decarbonization and digital economy transitions, particularly in the EU, where dependency on imports from China remains a strategic vulnerability.

Lithium, critical for battery production, supports the EU's decarbonization goals and the global shift toward electric mobility. Ukraine's reserves offer an alternative to China's dominance in lithium processing, in line with Europe's efforts to diversify supply chains through the European Battery Alliance.

In this context, Ukraine's unique role in the global raw material eco-system is accompanied by Russia's ongoing territorial ambitions.

Despite significant challenges, Ukraine has decisively worked to decouple from its communist past, implementing reforms that align with democratic values and market-driven principles. These efforts have positioned the nation as a forward-looking, modern, and dynamic economy.

Finalizing Ukraine's decoupling from its Soviet inheritance, inher-ently linked to resisting external imperialistic ambitions, and unlocking its unique resource potential, require bold leadership, forward-thinking policies, and coordinated international collaboration. The EU's empha-sis on supply chain integration, paired with Ukraine's commitment to modernization and alignment with EU and global standards, establishes a robust platform for such a forward-looking partnership. For stake-holders aiming to invest in Ukraine or secure their position in the global resource ecosystem, the strategic imperative is to position Ukraine's resource base as a strategic asset for security, defense, and the digital economy.

II. Evaluating Ukraine's Investment Attractiveness through the Sectoral Lens

Macroeconomic stability provides the foundation for FDI, but realizing Ukraine's—or any nation's—full potential demands a sectoral analysis that identifies actionable opportunities. This approach evaluates three critical dimensions: trade dynamics with key partners, strategic insights from leading investors, and sector contribution and level of integration with global supply chains. By synthesizing these factors, the analysis re-veals high-impact opportunities across sectors, shaping Ukraine's appeal to the global investment community.

Strategic Sectors with Unique Stories: Ukraine's Role in Global Supply Chains

Ukraine's export portfolio reflects its foundational role in global supply chains, with a structure heavily weighted toward essential agricultural commodities and raw materials. This composition presents Ukraine's current economic identity and its strategic significance to international trade. By evaluating these sectors through the lens of global integration and trade dynamics with key partners, Ukraine stands as a critical supplier in sustaining vital industries worldwide. Its contributions span agriculture, metals, chemicals, and industrial goods—sectors that anchor global supply chains. Within these, Ukraine ranks among the world's leading exporters, leveraging its natural resources and industrial capacity to deliver critical products that contribute to global security.

1. **Agriculture: A Strategic Lever for Global Food Security**

Ukraine's agricultural sector stands as a cornerstone of global food security, uniquely positioned by its unparalleled natural assets and historical significance as a leading exporter. The fertile black soil, covering over 70 percent of the country, provides the foundation for Ukraine's agricultural productivity, enabling it to rank among the world's top exporters of wheat, corn, barley, and sunflower oil. This natural endowment supports not only high yields but also exceptional quality, making Ukraine an indispensable supplier to markets across Europe, Asia, and Africa.

In 2023 despite the conflict, Ukraine remained the European Union's third-largest source of agrifood imports by value, contributing cereals (21.9 percent of total imports), vegetable and seed oils (17.4 percent), and a wide array of agricultural products. Beyond these staples, Ukraine's export portfolio includes honey, where it is a top-five global supplier, as well as dried peas and chicken meat—key commodities for both human consumption and livestock feed. These diverse offerings underscore the sector's strategic importance, and its resilience amid geopolitical and logistical challenges.

The significance of Ukraine's agricultural sector is further underscored by its role in stabilizing global food markets. Wheat, corn, and barley account for nearly 35 percent of Ukraine's total exports, and sunflower oil export volumes solidify the nation's position as the world's largest supplier. These exports are critical inputs for food processing industries worldwide, ensuring steady supply chains and price stability. Key trading partners, including Egypt, China, India, and EU nations such as Italy, Spain, and the Netherlands, rely heavily on Ukrainian agriculture to meet their food security needs.

Strategic FDI in advanced farming technologies, storage infrastructure, and supply chain modernization can catalyze transformative growth, amplifying Ukraine's capacity to meet global demand. Investments in these areas will address immediate reconstruction needs while positioning Ukraine as a leader in sustainable agriculture. By fostering resilience and innovation, targeted FDI can strengthen Ukraine's role in ensuring global food security. Moreover, it is essential to embed sustainability as an FDI element to confront the dual challenges of climate change and postwar demining, secure stability in global supply chains, and advance social cohesion in interconnected markets.

2. The Strategic Edge of Ukraine's Chemical Sector: Unlocking Its Sustainability Potential

Ukraine's chemical sector is well-positioned to address global challenges—from enhancing agricultural productivity to advancing manufacturing. Anchored by abundant reserves of sulfur, natural gas, and other critical raw materials, the sector operates on a strong foundation that minimizes reliance on imports and enables vertical integration. Decades of expertise in nitrogen-based fertilizer production have elevated Ukraine from a mere supplier of agricultural commodities to a unique enabler of advanced farming practices worldwide.

Its geographic position between Europe and Asia transforms it into a critical hub for trade and industrial connectivity. This location allows seamless access to Western and Eastern markets, with the EU—particularly Germany, Poland, and Italy—remaining the core destination. Turkey's substantial imports further underscore the sector's role in supporting agricultural productivity across the Black Sea region. Beyond the EU, major importers such as China, India, Egypt, and Saudi Arabia rely on Ukrainian chemical products to sustain their agricultural and manufacturing sectors' needs.

Despite these strengths, the sector faces challenges, including wartime damage and the need for technological upgrades. Yet, these challenges also present opportunities. Targeted investments can expand Ukraine's production capacity, restore infrastructure, and align the industry with global decarbonization goals. With its vast natural resources, strategic location, and potential for technological advancement, Ukraine's chemical sector is poised to get an additional competitive edge.

3. Metals and Mining: A Historically Important Sector Ripe for Transformation

Ukraine's metals and mining sector, for long a cornerstone of its industrial economy, is underpinned by some of the world's most significant reserves of iron ore, titanium, manganese, and zircon. These resources position Ukraine as a critical supplier to Europe, accounting for over 75 percent of the EU's nonferrous metal and steel imports—essential inputs for construction, automotive, and energy industries. Beyond volume, titanium and zirconium exports are indispensable for high-precision applications in aerospace and renewable energy technologies, where performance and material reliability are critical. Key export destinations include the EU (notably Germany, Poland, and Italy), Turkey, and China.

In 2023, the metallurgical sector accounted for 17.8 percent of Ukraine's industrial output and 23.5 percent of total export revenues. While this reflects its significance to the national economy and provides essential export income, this reliance constrains Ukraine's growth trajectory and perpetuates its position at the lower end of the value chain. To achieve its aspirations for accelerated GDP growth and sustained global competitiveness, Ukraine must rethink its approach. Prioritizing value-added production—such as advanced alloys, precision-engineered components, and finished goods—will allow the nation to capture greater economic value, reduce risks inherent in commodity-driven markets, and align with its ambition for accelerated economic growth.

This shift is not merely economic—it represents a strategic imperative. Moving up the value chain will require targeted investments in industrial modernization, technology, and workforce development, coupled with policies designed to attract private capital and foster technological advancement. By repositioning its metals and mining sector as a driver of industrial sophistication rather than a raw material supplier, Ukraine can unlock untapped economic potential and align with global trends favoring sustainability and high-value production.

4. Machinery and Machine Building Sector

While Ukraine's economic narrative is largely shaped by strategically integrated, high-export-revenue sectors that dominate global supply chains—such as agriculture, metals, and chemicals—industries with moderate growth potential warrant attention. Among these is the machinery and machine-building sector—a historically significant contributor to Ukraine's industrial economy. Although it does not currently rank among the nation's top growth drivers, this sector remains vital due to its contribution to export revenues, its role in domestic industrial capacity, and its potential to support critical infrastructure. Capital investments from the state and Development Finance Institutions can support modernization and efficiency, ensuring this sector continues to play a supportive role in Ukraine's broader economic strategy.

Historically a cornerstone of Ukraine's industrial economy, the machinery sector now grapples with aging infrastructure and reliance on outdated Soviet-era technologies, constraining efficiency and global competitiveness. Despite these limitations, the sector accounts for approximately 8 percent of Ukraine's export revenue, with key markets including Poland, Germany, and Romania. Before 2022, Russia was a significant destination for high-demand products such as electrical motors, food processing lines, and aviation components.

Positioned within the Fourth Technological Mode, the sector produces a diverse range of export goods, including technical and electrical equipment for nuclear reactors, boilers, turbines, compressors, trains and locomotives, and machinery for food processing and packaging. IMF assessments underscore the sector's moderate growth potential, contingent on strategic investments in modernization, R&D, and production efficiency. Unlocking this potential requires a combination of domestic and foreign direct investment, prioritizing upgrades to production capabilities, adoption of advanced technologies, and integration into global supply chains. Government support—through tax incentives, public-private partnerships, and targeted FDI—can support technological transformation and enhance export potential, particularly in niche markets and export-driven subsectors.

Understanding MNC Investment Motivations:
A Sectoral Analysis of Ukraine's Economic Appeal

What drives multinational corporations to invest in Ukraine? A sectoral analysis reveals diverse motivations, where industries offer varying levels of appeal shaped by distinct returns, strategic priorities, and the unique opportunities presented by Ukraine's national economy.

Table 5.19 Structure of FDI inflows

Strategic investor group	Percentage of total FDI inflows (2014)	Percentage of total FDI inflows (2020)
Multinational corporations (MNCs)	62	57
Private investors	15	20
Development finance institutions (DFIs)	10	12
State-owned enterprises	8	7
Others	5	4
Total	100	100

The FDI structure highlights the dominance of global multinational corporations (MNCs), which account for up to 70 percent of investment stock in Ukraine. Table 5.19 details the percentage of total FDI inflows attributed to each group across the analyzed years.

Since its transition to a market economy in 1991, Ukraine has emerged as a compelling investment destination, attracting global giants such as ArcelorMittal, Cargill, Syngenta, Procter & Gamble, Coca-Cola, Danone, Nestlé, Carlsberg, Anheuser-Busch InBev, Saint-Gobain, Kraft Foods, and others. Drawn by Ukraine's rich resource endowment and competitive workforce, these corporations have pursued investments that are in line with their broader strategies of market expansion and supply chain optimization.

Ukraine's steadfast commitment to market reforms and the liberalization of economic policies have further enhanced its appeal to multinational corporations (MNCs). Large MNCs have targeted sectors where Ukraine holds a strong position in global supply chains, leveraging its strategic advantages to secure operational efficiencies and expand market reach.

The agricultural sector exemplifies this dynamic. Ukraine's status as the EU's largest agrifood supplier and its critical role in stabilizing global food markets are widely acknowledged by MNCs. Leading agribusinesses such as Cargill, Syngenta, and ADM capitalized on Ukraine's expansive production capabilities and logistics infrastructure to create stable and efficient supply chains for grains, oilseeds, and essential commodities. This investment momentum has been expanded by Ukraine's agricultural land reforms, commitment to modernizing farming practices through technology adoption, and improvements in logistics infrastructure and export processes.

Ukraine's renewable energy potential has drawn the attention of global leaders such as EDF Renewables and Siemens Energy, positioning the country as an emerging strategic hub in Europe's decarbonization strategy. With wind energy potential estimated between 16 and 24 gigawatts—of which 16 gigawatts is already deemed economically viable—Ukraine offers a compelling opportunity to scale renewable energy projects in harmony with EU climate goals. When combined with its substantial solar resources, Ukraine's renewable energy sector positions the country as a unique frontier for scaling renewable energy projects in alignment with the European Union and UN Sustainable Development Goals.

Ukraine's integration into the European energy grid, and a suite of favorable policy measures, further elevated its position as a high-potential energy market. Yet, the country's energy appeal extends beyond renewables. Ukraine operates 15 nuclear reactors, placing it seventh globally in nuclear power capacity and making it a critical player in the nuclear energy ecosystem. The United States, operating 94 nuclear reactors and with the most recent facility opened in 2024, has a longstanding partnership with Ukraine's nuclear sector. A notable example is the US$30 billion agreement between Ukraine's Energoatom and U.S.-based Westinghouse Electric Company to construct next-generation nuclear reactors using AP1000 technology.

Multinational corporations MNCs approach Ukraine with a blend of strategic imperatives that reveal both opportunity and calculated pragmatism. Two primary motivations dominate their approach. First, Ukraine serves as a strategic market for extending the lifecycle of products and technologies that have plateaued in advanced economies. By entering a less saturated market, MNCs unlock residual value from mature innovations, exemplifying the international product cycle's adaptability to diverse economic environments.

Second, Ukraine's regulatory environment—less stringent than that of the EU—provides operational flexibility. This is particularly noticeable in industries such as chemicals, food, and tobacco, where global players can deploy products that might fall short of stricter European standards. For MNCs, this creates a compelling cost–benefit dynamic: They capitalize on regulatory gaps while maintaining competitive positioning in high-growth markets.

However, this investment narrative reflects a dichotomy. While MNCs bring capital inflows and stimulate economic activity, their focus on market expansion often diverges from Ukraine's strategic priorities of technological modernization and high-value production. The macroeconomic implications are clear: Ukraine's investment appeal frequently caters to corporate objectives rather than fostering long-term national innovation capacity.

To recalibrate this alignment, Ukraine must attract entrepreneurial investors whose strategic interests coincide with its developmental ambitions. Policies aimed at channeling FDI into high-tech sectors, leveraging domestic scientific and technical expertise, and promoting collaborative innovation can transform investments into catalysts for sustainable growth.

Which Countries Are Leading the Way in Investing in Ukraine?

The full-scale Russian invasion in 2022 significantly disrupted foreign direct investment flows into Ukraine. Despite these challenges, Ukraine's indispensable role in global supply chains enabled it to attract critical capital inflows from international financial institutions (DFIs) and allied nations dedicated to supporting its economic resilience. Key sectors— energy, agriculture, and technology—became focal points for FDI, with investments targeting the reconstruction and modernization of vital infrastructure. The United States, the European Union, and Japan stood as a primary source of capital, directing several billion U.S. dollars toward initiatives that addressed both immediate stabilization and long-term recovery. DFIs proved pivotal during this period, not only driving reconstruction efforts but also ensuring the continuity of essential services under extraordinary circumstances.

In 2023, **the United States** ranked among the top sources of capital inflows, contributing approximately US$3.5 billion. Investments were strategically directed toward technology, energy, and defense—sectors

Table 5.20 Ukraine's GDP, capital investments, FDI, and financial aid

Year	GDP (US$ billion)	Total capital investments (US$ billion)	FDI (US$ billion)	Percentage share of FDI in total capital investment	Financial aid (US$ billion)
2010	136.0	47.3	6.5	13.7	2.0
2014	133.5	25.2	4.5	17.9	4.0
2020	155.6	30.5	3.3	10.8	3.5
2021	200.1	33.2	4.2	12.7	3.8
2022	130.8	20.4	3.2	15.7	8.5
2023*	132.0	22.0	3.5	15.9	12.0

Sources: Ukrainian State Statistical Committee: GDP, total capital investments, and FDI; Centre for Economic Strategy (CES): financial aid and official development from international financial institutions and foreign states. Data for 2023 is the estimate

critical to Ukraine's resilience and long-term competitiveness. The technology sector, with a focus on IT services and digital infrastructure, emerged as a key priority, reinforcing Ukraine's growing role in the global tech ecosystem and defense-related technological capacities. In the energy sector, U.S. investments targeted renewable energy projects and the modernization of Ukraine's energy grid, enhancing its capacity to withstand disruptions and strengthen energy security. The defense sector also garnered significant U.S. investment, including initiatives to enhance cybersecurity and sustain critical Internet infrastructure, reflecting a calibrated effort to strengthen Ukraine's defense capabilities to withstand the ongoing threats.

The European Union collectively directed US$3.2 billion to Ukraine in 2023, targeting infrastructure, energy, and agriculture. Infrastructure funding prioritized the restoration of war-damaged transportation networks and urban infrastructure, supporting connectivity and economic activities. In energy, EU investments balanced the immediate restoration of traditional energy systems with the strategic expansion of renewable energy capacity. Meanwhile, agriculture received substantial backing to secure Ukraine's critical role in protecting global food security and ensuring social stability in other vulnerable regions.

Germany, a key EU contributor, sustained its position as a notable investor in Ukraine, focusing on renewable energy, manufacturing, and infrastructure. In December 2023, following the escalation of conflict, Germany's Federal Ministry of Economic Affairs and Climate Action (BMWK), in partnership with the European Investment Bank (EIB), and Ukraine's Ministry for Restoration, announced a €20 million grant to integrate solar energy systems, biomass solutions, and geothermal heat pumps into schools and hospitals.

Beyond advancing renewable energy, Germany prioritized safeguarding Ukraine's energy infrastructure against Russia's ongoing missile assaults. Recognizing the urgent need to restore and protect energy facilities ahead of the harsh winter months, the German government committed €195 million in October 2023 and an additional €100 million in September 2024 to address vulnerabilities caused by sustained attacks. These actions reflect Germany's calibrated strategy to balance immediate humanitarian needs with longer-term energy security objectives—including grid stability, energy source diversification, and the stabilization of energy costs and supply.

Since 2014, when the conflict over Ukraine's Crimea and Donbas began, **Japan** has emerged as a critical partner in supporting Ukraine through initiatives executed by the United Nations Development Program (UNDP). Focused on comprehensive human security, Japan's aid has reached an estimated 6 million Ukrainians, targeting essential services such as heating, power supplies, health care, livelihood support, and rehabilitation.

By 2023, Japan had become the third-largest donor to Ukraine, contributing US$4.2 billion since the start of the full-scale Russian invasion in February 2022. On December 6, 2023, Prime Minister Fumio Kishida announced an additional US$4.5 billion in humanitarian and recovery aid, supporting projects such as access to clean water, sewage system stabilization, explosive ordnance clearance, debris removal, and rehabilitation for those affected by the war.

Japan's strategic motivation in aiding Ukraine is rooted in its commitment to defending international norms, safeguarding regional security, and reinforcing global stability. The territorial integrity of nations is a principle fundamental to global stability, and by supporting Ukraine, nations uphold the rule of law and deter similar violations elsewhere.

In November 2024, Japan was allocating US$7.46 billion to its fiscal investment and loan program targeting Ukraine's comprehensive rebuild. Japan's stance reflects its view of Russia's invasion as a direct challenge to the existing rules-based international order—a turning point that has disrupted geopolitical stability and marked the end of an era of unparalleled international cooperation and connectivity following the dissolution of the Soviet Union.

The Japanese government has drawn parallels between Russia's actions in Ukraine and potential threats in East Asia, particularly concerning North Korea and regional tensions. Japan emphasizes that instability in one region can reverberate across global markets and security dynamics, highlighting the need for a collective commitment to preserving a rules-based international order.

Understanding which nations lead the FDI process in Ukraine, along with their strategic motivations, scale, and sectoral allocation of funds, provides a critical lens for crafting long-term partnerships. These insights help to identify shared values and objectives while informing the design of an investment strategy aligned with Ukraine's national growth goals, addressing immediate challenges such as safeguarding critical sectors while enabling restoration and sustainable growth.

Identifying reliable economic and strategic partners committed to accelerating Ukraine's recovery is key to shaping effective FDI strategies and attraction mechanisms. Such strategies must balance immediate domestic priorities with global geopolitical dynamics and long-term economic and social megatrends. For policy makers, the distribution of international support offers valuable guidance to align national objectives with global frameworks, laying the groundwork for a forward-thinking and resilient economic strategy.

Shaping an FDI-Driven Recovery

Ukraine faces immense challenges on its path to recovery. The ongoing devastation wrought by Russia's aggression has inflicted profound damage—not only to Ukraine's physical infrastructure—and has complicated economic foundations and the country's global integration prospects. The scale of destruction is staggering: The reconstruction of housing, infrastructure, energy systems, transportation networks, and agricultural land has required over a decade of restoration projects and billions in investments. Debris clearance and explosive hazard management costs are nearing US$11 billion, and landmines clearing will require an additional US$34.6 billion.

The next step in leveraging FDI as a growth mechanism involves a rigorous evaluation of sectoral investment potential from the perspective of Ukraine's long-term development strategy. This process identifies sectors with dual purposes—(1) those that serve as pathways for economic recovery and (2) those that support Ukraine's future global competitiveness. It identifies diversification opportunities by analyzing sector growth patterns and the country's economic structure (Table 5.21).

Information Technology (IT) and Digital Services: Ukraine's IT sector stands out due to its robust growth and innovation. The country benefits from a large pool of highly skilled IT professionals and competitive labor costs, making it a favorable destination for tech investments. The World Bank highlights Ukraine's increasing role as a tech hub, supported by a burgeoning startup ecosystem and a growing emphasis on digital transformation. Russia's full-scale war against Ukraine has devastated the nation's economy, shrinking GDP by over 30 percent in 2022. Yet, amid the turmoil, Ukraine's digital technology and creative startup sector has defied the odds, emerging as the only export-focused industry to achieve growth during the conflict. In 2022 alone, IT exports generated US$6.8 billion, and during the 12 months following Russia's invasion, the sector surpassed US$7.34 billion in export revenues—a 5 percent increase from the previous year. This remarkable performance, sustaining 285,000 skilled jobs, proves the inherent resilience and innovation embedded in Ukraine's tech ecosystem.

Before the war, Ukraine's technology sector demonstrated exponential growth, expanding 38 percent between 2020 and 2021 to reach nearly US$7 billion in export revenue. Today, this momentum continues, fueled by highly skilled and motivated talent and the inflow of graduates eager to participate in cutting-edge segments such as defense tech, cybersecurity, and emerging technology solutions. Ukrainian tech talent, already acknowledged by global tech powerhouses for its creativity and innovation, has positioned the nation as a digital hub. A global client base,

Table 5.21 Sectoral attractiveness as defined by top investors

Investment priority	Sectors	Commentary
High attractiveness	IT and digital services	Ukraine's IT sector is highly competitive due to a strong pool of tech talent, low operational costs, and a growing startup ecosystem. Recent investments from international tech firms bolster this (JETCO, Netherlands, China)
	Agriculture	Strong export and strong competitive position in food supply chains. Reforms, enhanced infrastructure, and new agri-practices raise sector efficiency and investment appeal. The country's fertile soil and extensive arable land offer opportunities in crop production, agribusiness, and food processing (UNCTAD, Netherlands, Germany)
	Renewable energy	Significant potential in solar and wind energy, supported by favorable policies, international climate commitments, and growing capital allocations from DFIs (IMF, World Bank, Netherlands, China)
	Infrastructure and logistics	Strategic location as a trade corridor with investments needed in infrastructure. Both domestic and foreign investments focus on improving logistics capabilities (JETCO, World Bank, Germany)
Moderate attractiveness	Manufacturing and machine building	The sector faces challenges such as outdated facilities but offers opportunities for modernization. Investment interest is growing but is tempered by operational and regulatory challenges (IMF, JETCO, Germany)
	Chemicals, petrochemicals	The sector presents opportunities but is affected by market volatility, environmental regulations, and competition. Investment is cautious due to these factors (UNCTAD, Netherlands, DFIs)
	Pharma	110 licensed manufacturers, employing approximately 23,000 personnel, compound annual growth rate (CAGR) of 11.5%, export-oriented
	Fintech	With over 240 fintech companies, the landscape is diverse, encompassing areas such as payments, lending, and technological infrastructure. State support aims to further enhance sector attractiveness
Low attractiveness	Conventional power generation	High capital requirements and transition to no-carbon make it less attractive compared to renewables (World Bank, Netherlands, DFIs)

with 95 percent being overseas and established long before the war, has fortified the sector against domestic disruptions and positioned it as an indispensable part of Europe's technology ecosystem. With the resilience test passed, the sector emerged stronger.

As global competition for tech talent intensifies, Ukraine's workforce stands out for its capacity to drive innovation and creativity. Even modest capital injections yield returns; for example, US$1.2 million in U.S. direct assistance generated US$12.2 million in sales and attracted US$5.9 million in private sector investments. How might defense-related innovation further reshape global technological leadership?

Energy: Powering Progress through Renewable Potential: The Energy Sector, particularly green energy, remains a key focus as it is a critical foundation for national stability and resilience. Investors are increasingly recognizing Ukraine's green energy sector as a market with substantial growth potential and strategic importance.

Energy security and renewable development are essential to Ukraine's strategy for economic independence. With vast wind, solar, and bioenergy resources, Ukraine holds the potential to become a notable contributor to Europe's sustainable energy ambitions. Before the conflict, Ukraine had already made meaningful progress in renewable energy development. Today, the urgency for FDI in energy infrastructure is even more pressing. Investments in renewable energy projects, energy-efficient systems, and grid modernization can accelerate Ukraine's energy transition, reduce reliance on Russian energy, and support Europe's broader objectives for energy security and resilience. In August 2024, the Ukrainian government presented a plan to increase the share of renewable energy to 27 percent in the national energy mix, requiring US$20 billion in investments by 2030. FDI inflows into solar and wind energy projects could be further increased through supportive government policies.

Infrastructure, networks, and construction: The ongoing conflict has extensively damaged Ukraine's infrastructure, creating an urgent need for investment in reconstruction, particularly in transportation, housing, and utilities. In collaboration with international partners, the Ukrainian government has developed a strategic framework for postwar recovery. This includes the establishment of the U.S.–Ukraine Infrastructure Task

Force, designed to address both immediate wartime needs and future reconstruction priorities.

Several international partners and allies have already begun making notable allocations. Italy, undeterred by the ongoing conflict, allocated €200 million to reconstruction. The Netherlands has prioritized investments in infrastructure, residential housing, and drinking water facilities. The Dutch government provides support, including assistance and grants, to companies considering business with Ukraine. The focus is on sectors where Dutch expertise can provide the greatest added value: agriculture, water management, and health care. Denmark has implemented a fast-track system to expedite Danish investment in Ukraine's reconstruction, leading efforts in rebuilding war-torn regions. Japan hosted the inaugural Japan–Ukraine Conference for the Promotion of Economic Growth and Reconstruction, convening over 80 leading Japanese companies. The initiative resulted in cooperation and partnership agreements.

These early investments and partnership agreements demonstrate a nascent global consensus on priority sectors and required allocations. Sustaining this momentum demands a cohesive strategy to stimulate higher levels of FDI.

Ukraine's FDI-driven model can set a global precedent for post-conflict national restoration and growth by demonstrating how reconstruction efforts can advance innovation, foster inclusivity, and embed sustainability at the heart of economic renewal.

5.5 Key Mechanisms to Stimulate Foreign Direct Investment in Ukraine's Strategic Sectors

This chapter investigates key mechanisms employed by governments worldwide to attract and optimize FDI, synthesizing insights from academic research, strategic reports, and best practices from leading donor nations. By combining universally applicable strategies with contextual adaptations tailored to Ukraine's economic landscape, it offers an evidence-based framework for enhancing investment inflows.

Overview of Mechanisms

1. **Development of a Comprehensive Investment Strategy**
   A coherent national, sectoral, and regional investment strategy forms the backbone of any successful FDI attraction plan. Such a strategy should articulate investment priorities, align with national economic objectives, and address sector-specific challenges. Without a well-defined framework, countries risk ad hoc investment decisions, short-termism, and heightened vulnerability to shifts in global dynamics. A robust investment strategy ensures balanced development, fosters resilience to global economic shifts, and establishes a competitive edge in attracting high-quality investments.

2. **Improvement of the Legal and Regulatory Framework**
   A transparent and efficient legal framework is critical to fostering investor confidence. Streamlining regulations, safeguarding property rights, and minimizing bureaucratic hurdles are foundational steps toward creating a business-friendly environment. Legal reforms should prioritize alignment with international standards, reducing uncertainty and risks for foreign investors. These measures not only increase predictability but also enhance the overall investment climate, positioning the country as a reliable destination for FDI.

3. **Marketing and Promotion of Investment Opportunities**

   Successful FDI attraction relies on targeted marketing and promotion strategies. Successful government strategies include targeted promotional campaigns, leveraging international forums, and showcasing a compelling narrative about a country's competitive advantages. Sectoral success stories and data-driven approaches to identify and engage potential investors further amplify the effectiveness of these campaigns.

4. **Provision of Incentives and Benefits**

   Tailored incentives significantly enhance a country's appeal to foreign investors. These incentives may include tax breaks, financial subsidies, streamlined approval processes, and preferential treatment in high-priority sectors. Designing these benefits to align with national development goals ensures that FDI not only flows in but also contributes meaningfully to the national economy's long-term growth.

5. **Political and Economic Stability**

   A stable political and economic environment is indispensable for attracting and sustaining FDI. Good governance, transparency, anticorruption measures, and effective economic risk management, including state insurance, instill confidence among investors. Predictability in macroeconomic policy and political stability directly influence the feasibility and attractiveness of long-term investment projects.

6. **Strengthening Infrastructure and Human Capital**

   High-quality infrastructure and skilled labor are a strong contributor to a country's investment appeal. Transportation networks, reliable utilities, and digital infrastructure enhance businesses' operational efficiency. Simultaneously, targeted investments in education and vocational training improve workforce productivity, drive innovation, and address sector-specific needs, making the economy and specific sectors more appealing to foreign investors.

7. **Integration into the Global Economy**

   Integration into global trade networks and adherence to international standards can significantly enhance a country's FDI attractiveness and signal commitment to openness and reliability. This involves active participation in trade agreements, promotion of cross-border collaboration, and aligning domestic practices with global standards. Ukraine's proximity to major markets positions it to capitalize on such integration, boosting its global competitiveness.

By adopting these practices, Ukraine can significantly enhance its attractiveness to investors and lay the foundation for sustainable, long-term development across its key economic sectors.

An effective investment strategy should prioritize the following:

- Developing a comprehensive strategic framework at the national, sectoral, and regional levels;
- Strengthening the legal and regulatory framework governing FDIs;
- Implementing a targeted marketing approach to enhance the appeal of industries and regions to potential investors.

Research into the management of foreign investment identifies four key priority areas that host countries typically focus on when attracting FDI.

Strategic priorities of recipient countries in attracting FDI

Directions and goals of attracting FDI		Directions			
		Financial and economic	Production and technical	Organizational and managerial	Political
Goals	1. Addressing financial deficits	Compensating for internal financial shortfalls	Attracting advanced technologies	Facilitating the transfer of cutting-edge technologies into the country	Promoting global integration
	2. Stimulating economic development	Accelerating economic growth by developing industries that supply products to sectors receiving FDI	Developing fundamentally new production facilities	Establishing new manufacturing sites to expand capacity	Providing incentives to political allies
		Development of related and adjacent industries to create a network effect	Supporting high-tech industries	Fostering the growth of technology-driven sectors	Benefits and preferences for FDI from countries that are political partners

Ukraine's investment strategy for attracting foreign capital should focus on creating favorable conditions for both foreign investors and domestic counterparts. The strategy must prioritize long-term investment projects that reinvest profits and target sectors critical to national development and growth. It should strike a balance between economic openness—a key aspect of global integration—and reasonable protectionism in industries essential to national security. This involves fostering domestic production, improving social well-being and living standards, and establishing mechanisms to protect against external threats. A well-defined strategy must also articulate sectoral and regional priorities to channel foreign capital effectively.

The development of Ukraine's investment strategy can proceed through four key stages, each designed to align foreign investment with the country's long-term goals and achieve its growth targets.

Four Key Stages in Investment Strategy Designs

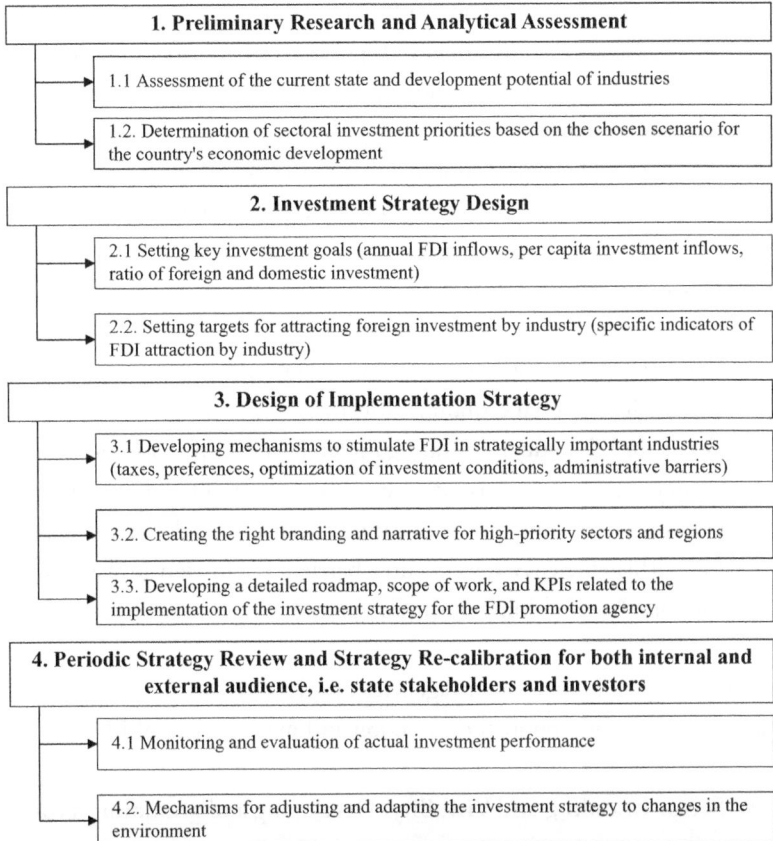

1. Preliminary Research and Analytical Assessment

1.1 Assessment of the current state and development potential of industries

1.2. Determination of sectoral investment priorities based on the chosen scenario for the country's economic development

2. Investment Strategy Design

2.1 Setting key investment goals (annual FDI inflows, per capita investment inflows, ratio of foreign and domestic investment)

2.2. Setting targets for attracting foreign investment by industry (specific indicators of FDI attraction by industry)

3. Design of Implementation Strategy

3.1 Developing mechanisms to stimulate FDI in strategically important industries (taxes, preferences, optimization of investment conditions, administrative barriers)

3.2. Creating the right branding and narrative for high-priority sectors and regions

3.3. Developing a detailed roadmap, scope of work, and KPIs related to the implementation of the investment strategy for the FDI promotion agency

4. Periodic Strategy Review and Strategy Re-calibration for both internal and external audience, i.e. state stakeholders and investors

4.1 Monitoring and evaluation of actual investment performance

4.2. Mechanisms for adjusting and adapting the investment strategy to changes in the environment

Establishing Sector-Specific Investment Agencies: A Governance Mechanism for Strategic Delivery

An important governance mechanism to ensure the effective implementation of investment strategy is the establishment and effective functioning of a sector-specific investment agency. This approach has proven successful in many developing economies, where tailored agencies have been instrumental in attracting and managing foreign direct investments. The key advantages of such an agency include:

1. **Centralized Management:** A dedicated agency serves as a centralized hub for FDI processes, offering investors streamlined access to transparent, reliable, and up-to-date information. By aggregating and disseminating investment proposals from industry enterprises, it simplifies data-gathering and supports the decision-making process for potential investors. The agency should design a global branding strategy highlighting Ukraine's unique strengths—such as its strategic location, skilled workforce, and emerging tech sector—and promote a nation as a premier investment destination.

2. **Consistency and Clear Structure:** The agency executes comprehensive strategies to attract investment and promote specific sectors internationally, ensuring a structured and cohesive approach that aligns with national economic priorities.

3. **Focus on Efficiency:** Operating under a "one-stop shop" model, the agency reduces administrative burdens by simplifying critical processes such as company registration, licensing, and obtaining permits. This efficiency lowers entry barriers for foreign investors and supports "ease of doing business."

Sector-specific investment agencies are designed to fulfill key functions that directly support the attraction and management of FDI:

1. **Sector Branding and Visibility:** Developing and promoting a compelling narrative for the sector to position it as a competitive and attractive destination for foreign investment. Facilitate partnerships between foreign investors and national innovation ecosystems to promote co-development of technology and talent and connect investors with local accelerators and R&D centers.

2. **Identifying Strategic Groups of Investors:** Proactively identifying and engaging foreign companies with the potential to undertake promising investment projects, creating mutually beneficial partnerships. Connect investors with public sector opportunities,

streamlining the Public-Private Partnership PPP process, and promote these collaborations internationally.

3. **Facilitating Investor Engagement:** Organizing tailored investor visits to enable foreign companies to explore opportunities, assess project viability, and connect with local stakeholders. Focusing not just on project-level support but also on fostering enduring relationships with investors to encourage reinvestment and sustained engagement.

4. **Providing Strategic Guidance:** Supporting investors through a structured decision-making process, including the development of roadmaps that outline the stages of launching and scaling investment projects, from market entry to achieving profitability. Post-investment support should keep in focus reinvestment opportunities and programs.

5. **Monitoring and Recalibration:** Continuously overseeing the implementation of investment projects, identifying challenges, and making necessary adjustments to ensure their success. Acting as a bridge between investors and government entities, the agency can advocate for regulatory reforms that enhance the investment climate and address barriers to entry.

The state should ensure there is a capacity-building program for agency staff to improve their expertise in negotiation, sector-specific knowledge, and investor relations.

Guiding Principles for Increasing FDI Inflows

To enhance foreign direct investment inflows and stimulate national economic growth, a nation must adhere to several guiding principles that strategically target investment, foster an attractive business environment, and ensure alignment with national priorities.

1. **Prioritize Key Sectors:** The investment strategy should identify and prioritize sectors and areas for development that are attractive to foreign investors. This includes sectors that are not only beneficial from a national-interest perspective but also offer significant potential

for joint ventures. Sectors critical to the country's economic development should receive favorable investment conditions, especially those with high national priority but less favorable economic conditions, to stimulate foreign capital inflow.

2. **Align Investor and National Interests:** Developing a regulatory framework for foreign investors necessitates a thorough understanding of how investor objectives align with the host country's priorities. Defining "bona fide investments"—where mutual interests converge—is critical to fostering sustainable collaboration. Investment projects should be assessed for their alignment with the country's socioeconomic development goals and their potential to advance national interests. Projects that meet these criteria and demonstrate long-term value should be prioritized with targeted incentives and guarantees.

3. **Emphasize Long-Term Orientation and Reinvestment:** Investment projects should focus on long-term goals and substantial profit reinvestment, ensuring sustained economic benefits and alignment with Ukraine's strategic development objectives.

4. **Promote Job Creation and Economic Integration:** FDI should contribute to job creation within investee companies and the broader Ukrainian economy. Investments should utilize local raw materials, components, and equipment, supporting domestic industries and reducing import dependence.

5. **Enhance Export Potential:** Investments should aim to boost Ukraine's export capabilities, strengthen the country's position in global markets, and contribute to economic stability and growth.

6. **Support Technological and Innovative Development:** Encouraging investments in modern, resource-saving, and environmentally friendly technologies is crucial. FDI should promote technological advancements and innovation within Ukraine, contributing to the country's development as a hub for modern technologies.

7. **Develop Ukrainian Trademarks and Technologies:** FDI should support the growth and internationalization of Ukrainian trademarks and technologies, fostering a stronger national brand and enhancing the global competitiveness of Ukrainian products and services.

8. **Reduce Economic Imbalances:** Investment strategies should aim to reduce inter-industry and inter-regional disparities within Ukraine, contributing to more equitable economic development across the country.

9. **Address Systemic Obstacles:** Recognize that increased foreign investment results from economic recovery rather than being its cause. Systemic obstacles—such as legal, economic, scientific, technological, and financial barriers—must be addressed to create a more favorable investment climate.

By adhering to these principles, Ukraine, or any other nation, can create a conducive environment for foreign investment, align investor interests with national development goals, and foster sustainable economic growth.

It is important to recognize that the growth of foreign investment should be viewed as a consequence of economic recovery rather than its primary driver. In Ukraine, systemic obstacles—encompassing legal, economic, scientific, technological, and financial challenges—hinder the realization of investment priorities.

To effectively attract foreign investment, Ukraine must implement targeted regulatory measures designed to address the diverse needs of investor groups while safeguarding national economic interests. Drawing from established economic theories, including the principles of market efficiency and risk management, the following measures are critical to enhancing foreign investment inflows:

Tax Incentives with Conditionality: Reducing the tax burden for enterprises with foreign investments that meet specific developmental criteria—such as exceeding defined investment thresholds, creating jobs, or contributing to priority sectors—can stimulate long-term economic growth. Theories of fiscal policy suggest that targeted tax incentives maximize resource allocation and reduce inefficiencies by channeling investments into sectors that yield the greatest societal benefit.

Capital Repatriation Policies: Implementing balanced capital repatriation policies that include moderate time delays and limits on profit repatriation ensures that foreign capital remains within the economy long enough to drive reinvestment and growth. While restrictive measures should avoid deterring investors, the Keynesian perspective emphasizes the role of retained capital in maintaining liquidity and stimulating aggregate demand.

Guarantees and Risk Mitigation: Establishing a comprehensive framework for risk insurance and loan guarantees for foreign investors can significantly reduce perceived investment risks. Supported by robust public-private partnerships, this aligns with modern financial intermediation theories, which highlight the importance of risk-sharing mechanisms in attracting high-value investments.

Enhanced Transparency and Public Accountability: Introducing mechanisms for public oversight of foreign investments made under preferential terms is crucial. This includes ensuring compliance with investment commitments, holding public officials accountable for managing these investments, and increasing transparency through publicly accessible reports. Institutional economics underscore the importance of transparency and accountability in reducing information asymmetry and fostering investor confidence.

Rigorous Investment Screening: It is essential to institute mandatory screening processes to evaluate the origin, reliability, and long-term viability of investments. This includes assessing the credibility of investor firms, requiring proof of operational stability, and imposing additional safeguards for preferential treatment. In line with screening models used in other economies, such as the Committee on Foreign Investment in the United States (CFIUS), this ensures alignment with national security and economic stability objectives.

A country's ability to attract FDI is measured by its capacity to deliver economic stability, execute a strategic investment promotion plan, and provide efficient institutional support. Drawing on economic theories and best practices from global leaders, the following measures prove to be effective:

1. **Economic Stability and Predictability:** A stable economic environment is paramount for attracting FDI. Investors seek predictable macroeconomic conditions, including controlled inflation,

sustainable fiscal policies, and consistent growth prospects. Trust and transparency reduce the cost of doing business and amplify investor confidence, which is critical for sustaining long-term investments. Political stability and adherence to the rule of law further enhance investor confidence.

2. **Developing a comprehensive investment promotion strategy:.** This involves:

   ○ *Targeted Investor Services*: Providing tailored support before, during, and after project approval to meet investor expectations efficiently. This approach mirrors successful practices in countries that are leading recipients of foreign capital. Studies on investor behavior reveal that investors respond positively to personalized approaches, streamlined project approvals, and transparency.

   ○ *Administrative Barrier Reduction*: Utilizing analytical techniques to identify and eliminate obstacles hindering investment, thereby streamlining processes and enhancing the ease of doing business.

   ○ *Brand Enhancement*: Improving the country's image among target investor groups through strategic marketing and communication efforts, ensuring that promotional activities are data-driven and effectively highlight competitive advantages. Behavioral economics suggests that emotional branding—aligning the nation's investment pitch with purpose-driven narratives, such as sustainability or technological innovation—resonates deeply with global investors.

3. **Institutional Mechanisms and Coordination:** Effective institutional support requires:

   ○ *Investment Facilitation Agencies*: Establishing dedicated agencies to centralize FDI processes, offering transparent and up-to-date information, and implementing comprehensive strategies to attract and retain investment.

   ○ *Public-Private Partnerships (PPPs)*: Facilitating PPPs to leverage private investment in public infrastructure projects, thereby sharing risks and benefits between the public and private sectors.

   ○ *Intergovernmental Coordination*: Ensuring cohesive actions among all public authorities, both horizontally across ministries and vertically between central and local governments, to present a unified and efficient investment framework. Countries such as Singapore have demonstrated how centralized, data-driven agencies catalyze high-value FDI inflows.

4. **Continuous Improvement and Stakeholder Engagement:** Engaging in ongoing dialogue with existing investors provides valuable insights into the investment climate, helping to identify and rectify deficiencies in current mechanisms and institutional support. This feedback loop is crucial for continuous improvement and is in line with practices observed in successful investment destinations. A dialogue with current investors is a goldmine of actionable insights. Ukraine should formalize structured feedback mechanisms to identify challenges, refine policies, and enhance investor satisfaction. Feedback loops reinforce trust, creating a ripple effect where satisfied investors advocate for the country globally.

5. **Sector-Specific Measures:** Ukraine possesses the foundational prerequisites to implement best practices in fostering its role as a global innovation hub. A highly skilled labor force with relatively low costs, a strong educational and scientific base, and robust computer and communications infrastructure create a fertile ground for strategic development. To capitalize on this potential, a focused effort to establish software and technology parks is essential. This includes forming domestic and international marketing initiatives to attract investment, fostering the growth of software-focused enterprises, and enacting stable, investor-friendly legislation.

A critical opportunity lies in co-financing investment projects that merge foreign financial resources with domestic expertise, laying the groundwork for the formation of Ukrainian multinational corporations and unicorns. These MNCs, supported by state policies offering selective tax incentives and promoting collaboration, can serve as engines for a competitive edge and economic resilience. By finding a balance between foreign MNCs and domestic entities, Ukraine can stimulate healthy market competition, enhance consumer satisfaction, and elevate the overall competitiveness of its economy.

Strategic sectors, such as defense and defense-related, aerospace, electronics, metallurgy, transportation, nuclear, and tech-driven segments, present the most promising prospects for founding Ukrainian unicorns and global corporations. Integrating the most successful enterprises into existing transnational alliances is another alternative that offers a dual advantage: leveraging foreign expertise while advancing indigenous technological and industrial capabilities. Alliances are particularly advantageous in high-tech sectors where Ukrainian firms can offer unique, cutting-edge developments, incentivizing global partnerships.

Capital Without Borders: FDI-Driven Growth Model for Strategic Advance

A robust investment strategy is more than a policy framework—it is the cornerstone of economic transformation, empowering Ukraine to align FDI with structural and technological modernization goals. To maximize FDI's transformative potential, Ukraine must prioritize long-term economic stability, innovation, and international competitiveness.

Three critical factors underpin Ukraine's sectoral investment priorities: the lifecycle stage and technological sophistication of industries, their contribution to economic stability, and their potential to enhance global competitiveness. This foundation enables the design of strategic scenarios:

1. **High-Tech Development:** Prioritizing aerospace, transport engineering, and defense-related sectors to foster innovation and global competitiveness.
2. **Competitive Industries:** Leveraging existing strengths in ferrous metallurgy, chemicals, and construction while diversifying for broader growth.
3. **Balanced Development:** Ensuring resilience through diversified investment across key sectors.

FDI's impact extends beyond capital infusion—it introduces advanced production techniques, modern management practices, and job creation, boosting tax and export revenues. A shift to quality-focused investments in high-tech and innovative sectors will drive sustainable growth, enhance the technological sophistication of all core sectors, and lay the groundwork for long-term economic resilience and social prosperity.

Finally, fostering Ukrainian MNCs is critical for economic sovereignty and global integration. By targeting high-potential sectors, Ukraine can modernize its economy and strengthen its global footprint.

The effectiveness of Ukraine's investment strategy hinges on addressing structural imbalances, fostering intergovernmental coordination, and implementing clear, actionable policies. By aligning foreign capital with national development priorities, Ukraine can secure its position as a competitive, resilient economy in the global marketplace.

Notes

1. N. Gregory Mankiw, *Macroeconomics*, 10th ed. (Worth Publishers, 2019).
2. OECD, *Benchmark Definition of Foreign Direct Investment*.
3. John Maynard Keynes, *The General Theory of Employment, Interest and Money* (Harcourt Brace, 1936).
4. Kiyoshi Kojima and Terutomo Ozawa, "Micro- and Macro-Economic Models of Direct Foreign Investment: Toward a Synthesis," *Hitotsubashi Journal of Economics* 25, no. 1 (June 1984).
5. Robert Z. Aliber, "A Theory of Direct Foreign Investment," in *The International Corporation: A Symposium*, ed. Charles P. Kindleberger (MIT Press, 1970).
6. Robert A. Mundell, "International Trade and Factor Mobility," *American Economic Review* 47, no. 3 (June 1957): 322.
7. John H. Dunning, *Explaining International Production* (Unwin Hyman, 1988).
8. John H. Dunning and Rajneesh Narula, eds., *Foreign Direct Investment and Governments: Catalysts for Economic Restructuring* (Routledge, 1996).
9. Gary Gereffi, "How to Make Global Supply Chains More Resilient," Columbia FDI Perspectives, No. 348, January 9, 2023.
10. Ricardo Hausmann et al., *The Atlas of Economic Complexity: Mapping Paths to Prosperity* (MIT Press, 2014); and Laura Alfaro, "The Absorptive Capacity of Developing Countries and the Role of FDI," Harvard Business School Working Paper No. 15-002 (2014).
11. Gita Gopinath, "Geopolitics and Its Impact on Global Trade and the Dollar" (IMF, 2024), https://www.imf.org/en/News/Articles/2024/05/07/sp-geopolitics-impact-global-trade-and-the-dollar-gita-gopinath; Stanford Center on China's Economy and Institutions, "Friendshoring? Nearshoring? Reshoring? How the U.S. Trade Relationship with China Is Evolving?" (Stanford University, 2022), https://sccei.fsi.stanford.edu/china-briefs/friendshoring-nearshoring-reshoring-how-us-trade-relationship-china-evolving; Raghuram Rajan, "'Friend-Shoring' Isn't Friendly" (Hoover Institution, 2022), https://www.hoover.org/research/friend-shoring-isnt-friendly.
12. Paul M. Romer, "Endogenous Technological Change," *Journal of Political Economy* 98, no. 5, Part 2 (October 1990): https://doi.org/10.1086/261725.
13. Yuval Noah Harari, "Why Technology Favors Tyranny," *Atlantic*, 2018, https://www.theatlantic.com/magazine/archive/2018/10/yuval-noah-harari-technology-tyranny/568330/.

14. United Nations Conference on Trade and Development, "World Investment Report 2023: Investing in Sustainable Energy for All" (United Nations, 2023), https://unctad.org/publication/world-investment-report-2023.

15. United Nations Conference on Trade and Development, "World Investment Report 2024: Investment Facilitation and Digital Government" (United Nations, 2024), https://unctad.org/publication/world-investment -report-2024.

16. Ian A. Cooper et al., "The Equity Home Bias Puzzle: A Survey," *Foundations and Trends in Finance* 7, no. 4 (2013): 289–416.

17. Martin Feldstein and Charles Horioka, "Domestic Saving and International Capital Flows," *Economic Journal* 90, no. 358 (1980): 314–29.

18. European Commission, "Commission Calls on Member States to Review Outbound Investments and Assess Risks to Economic Security," press release, January 15, 2025, https://ec.europa.eu/commission/presscorner /detail/en/ip_25_261.

19. Roy F. Harrod, "An Essay in Dynamic Theory," *Economic Journal* 49, no. 193 (1939): 14–33, https://doi.org/10.2307/2225181.

20. Evsey D. Domar, "Capital Expansion, Rate of Growth, and Employment," *Econometrica* 14, no. 2 (1946): 137–47, https://doi.org/10.2307/1905364.

21. Robert M. Solow, "A Contribution to the Theory of Economic Growth," *Quarterly Journal of Economics* 70, no. 1 (1956): 65–94, https://doi.org /10.2307/1884513.

22. Nicholas Kaldor, "A Model of Economic Growth," *Economic Journal* 67, no. 268 (1957): 591–624, https://doi.org/10.2307/2227704.

23. Joan Robinson, *The Accumulation of Capital* (Macmillan, 1956).

24. Romer, "Endogenous Technological Change," S71–S102.

25. Robert E. Lucas Jr., "On the Mechanics of Economic Development," *Journal of Monetary Economics* 22, no. 1 (1988): 3–42, https://doi.org /10.1016/0304-3932(88)90168-7.

26. Wassily Leontief, *Input-Output Economics*, 2nd ed. (Oxford University Press, 1986).

27. United Nations Conference on Trade and Development, "Foreign Direct Investment: Inward and Outward Flows and Stock, Annual." UNCTADstat Data Centre, accessed April 7, 2025, https://unctadstat.unctad.org /datacentre/dataviewer/US.FdiFlowsStock.

28. UNCTAD, "Foreign Direct Investment: Inward and Outward Flows and Stock, Annual."

29. Gross Fixed Capital Formation (GFCF) reflects the total value of long-term investments in productive physical assets such as machinery, infrastructure, and buildings. A sustained rise in GFCF is often interpreted as a signal of expanding production capacity and a forward-looking commitment to economic growth.

30. UNCTAD, "World Investment Report 2024."

31. World Bank Group, "State of Investment Promotion Agencies: Evidence from WAIPA–WBG's Joint Global Survey" (World Bank, 2020), https://documents1.worldbank.org/curated/en/499971594008431029/pdf/State-of-Investment-Promotion-Agencies-Evidence-from-WAIPA-WBG-s-Joint-Global-Survey.pdf.

32. *Investment and Innovation: Problems of Theory and Practice* (Institute for Economics and Forecasting of the Ukrainian Academy of Agrarian Sciences, 2003), 412.

Bibliography

Alfaro, Laura. "The Absorptive Capacity of Developing Countries and the Role of FDI." Harvard Business School Working Paper No. 15-002, 2014.

Aliber, Robert Z. "A Theory of Direct Foreign Investment." in *The International Corporation: A Symposium*, ed. Charles P. Kindleberger (MIT Press, 1970), 17–34.

American Chamber of Commerce in Poland. "Foreign Direct Investment in Poland." December 2020. Accessed April 7, 2025. https://swisschamber .pl/wp-content/uploads/2021/03/AmCham_IGCC-Foreign-Direct -Investment-in-Poland_F.pdf.

Association of Investment Promotion Agencies. "Website of the Association of Investment Promotion Agencies IPAnet" [electronic resource]. http://www .ipanet.net/.

Australian Government, Department of Industry, Science, Energy and Resources. "Modern Manufacturing Strategy." 2020. https://www.industry.gov.au /data-and-publications/modern-manufacturing-strategy.

Carr, David L., James R. Markusen, and Keith E. Maskus. "Estimating the Knowledge-Capital Model of the Multinational Enterprise." *American Economic Review* 91, no. 3 (June 2001): 693–708. https://doi.org/10.1257 /aer.91.3.693.

Cooper, Ian A., Piet Sercu, and Rosanne Vanpee. "The Equity Home Bias Puzzle: A Survey." *Foundations and Trends in Finance* 7, no. 4 (2013): 289–416.

CzechInvest. "Annual Reports and FDI Statistics." CzechInvest, 1992–2024.

Domar, Evsey D. "Capital Expansion, Rate of Growth, and Employment." *Econometrica* 14, no. 2 (1946): 137–47. https://doi.org/10.2307/1905364.

Dunning, John H. *Explaining International Production*. Unwin Hyman, 1988.

Dunning, John H., and Rajneesh Narula, eds. *Foreign Direct Investment and Governments: Catalysts for Economic Restructuring*. Routledge, 1996.

European Bank for Reconstruction and Development. "Transition Report 2023." EBRD, 2023.

European Commission. "Commission Calls on Member States to Review Outbound Investments and Assess Risks to Economic Security." Press release, January 15, 2025. https://ec.europa.eu/commission/presscorner/detail/en /ip_25_261.

European Union. "Ukraine Economic Overview and Investment Opportunities." European Commission, 2023.

Federal Ministry for Economic Affairs and Energy. "Industrial Strategy 2030: Guidelines for a German and European Industrial Policy." November 2019.

Fedulova, L. I. *Technological Development of the Ukrainian Economy.* Institute of Economics and Forecasting, 2006.

Feldstein, Martin, and Charles Horioka. "Domestic Saving and International Capital Flows." *Economic Journal* 90, no. 358 (1980): 314–29.

Gereffi, Gary. "How to Make Global Supply Chains More Resilient." Columbia FDI Perspectives, No. 348, January 9, 2023.

Gopinath, Gita. "Geopolitics and Its Impact on Global Trade and the Dollar." International Monetary Fund, 2024. https://www.imf.org/en/News/Articles/2024/05/07/sp-geopolitics-impact-global-trade-and-dollar-gita-gopinath.

Harari, Yuval Noah. "Why Technology Favors Tyranny." *Atlantic*, 2018. https://www.theatlantic.com/magazine/archive/2018/10/yuval-noah-harari-technology-tyranny/568330/.

Harrod, Roy F. "An Essay in Dynamic Theory." *Economic Journal* 49, no. 193 (1939): 14–33. https://doi.org/10.2307/2225181.

Harvard Business Review. *Strategies for Attracting Foreign Investment.* Harvard Business Publishing, 2024.

Hausmann, Ricardo, César A. Hidalgo, Sebastián Bustos, et al. *The Atlas of Economic Complexity: Mapping Paths to Prosperity.* MIT Press, 2014. Accessed April 6, 2025. https://growthlab.hks.harvard.edu/publications/atlas-economic-complexity-mapping-paths-prosperity.

International Finance Corporation. "Ukraine Investment Climate Report." IFC, 2022.

International Monetary Fund. "Global Investment Trends." IMF, 2024.

International Monetary Fund. *Balance of Payments and International Investment Position Manual.* 6th ed. IMF, 2009. https://www.imf.org/external/pubs/ft/bop/2007/pdf/bpm6.pdf.

International Trade Administration. "Committee on Foreign Investment in the United States (CFIUS)." Accessed April 8, 2025.

Investment and Innovation: Problems of Theory and Practice. Institute for Economics and Forecasting of the Ukrainian Academy of Agrarian Sciences, 2003.

Japan External Trade and Cooperation Organization. "Reports on Investment Opportunities in Ukraine." JETCO, 2023.

Japan External Trade Organization. "Japan's Global FDI Strategy." JETRO, 2019.

Japan External Trade Organization. "Invest Japan Report 2023." 2023.

Jimborean, Ramona, and Anna Kelber. "Foreign Direct Investment Drivers and Growth in Central and Eastern Europe in the Aftermath of the 2007 Global Financial Crisis." *Comparative Economic Studies* 59, no. 1 (March 2017): 23–54. https://doi.org/10.1057/s41294-016-0018-9.

Kaldor, Nicholas. "A Model of Economic Growth." *Economic Journal* 67, no. 268 (1957): 591–624. https://doi.org/10.2307/2227704.

Kearney. "The 2024 Kearney Foreign Direct Investment Confidence Index: Continued Optimism in the Face of Instability." Accessed April 7, 2025.

Keynes, John Maynard. *The General Theory of Employment, Interest and Money.* Harcourt Brace, 1936.

Kojima, Kiyoshi, and Terutomo Ozawa. "Micro- and Macro-Economic Models of Direct Foreign Investment: Toward a Synthesis." *Hitotsubashi Journal of Economics* 25, no. 1 (June 1984): 1–20.

Leontief, Wassily. *Input-Output Economics.* 2nd ed. Oxford University Press, 1986.

Lucas, Robert E., Jr. "On the Mechanics of Economic Development." *Journal of Monetary Economics* 22, no. 1 (1988): 3–42. https://doi.org /10.1016/0304-3932(88)90168-7.

Makogon, Y. V., V. I. Lyashenko, and V. A. Kravchenko. *Regional Economic Relations and Free Economic Zones: Textbook.* Donetsk, 2003.

Mankiw, N. Gregory. *Macroeconomics.* 10th ed. Worth Publishers, 2019.

Markusen, James R. *Multinational Firms and the Theory of International Trade.* MIT Press, 2002.

Ministry of Commerce of the People's Republic of China. "Statistical Bulletin of China's Outward and Inward Foreign Direct Investment 2022." MOFCOM, 2023a.

Ministry of Commerce of the People's Republic of China. "Statistical Bulletin of China's Outward and Inward Foreign Direct Investment." MOFCOM, various years.

Ministry of Commerce of the People's Republic of China. "China-Ukraine Economic and Trade Relations Report." MOFCOM, 2023b.

Mundell, Robert A. "International Trade and Factor Mobility." *American Economic Review* 47, no. 3 (June 1957): 321–35.

National Bank of Ukraine. "Main Indicators of Economic and Social Status of Ukraine in 2001–2006" [electronic resource]. Accessed April 7, 2025. http:// www.bank.gov.ua.

National Institute for Ukrainian-Russian Relations. "Formation and Development of Transnational Alliances in Ukraine" [electronic resource].

Naughton, Barry. *The Chinese Economy: Transitions and Growth.* MIT Press, 2007.

Netherlands Foreign Investment Agency. "Investment Climate Ukraine." NFIA, 2023.

Organisation for Economic Co-Operation and Development. *Benchmark Definition of Foreign Direct Investment.* 4th ed. OECD Publishing, 2008.

Organisation for Economic Co-Operation and Development. "OECD Economic Surveys: Slovak Republic 2014." OECD Publishing, November 2014.

https://www.oecd.org/content/dam/oecd/en/publications/reports/2014/11 /oecd-economic-surveys-slovak-republic-2014_g1g394f0/eco_surveys-svk -2014-en.pdf.

Organisation for Economic Co-Operation and Development. "OECD Economic Surveys: Poland 2014." OECD Publishing, March 2014. https://www.oecd .org/content/dam/oecd/en/publications/reports/2014/03/oecd-economic -surveys-poland-2014_g1g3942f/eco_surveys-pol-2014-en.pdf.

Organisation for Economic Co-Operation and Development. *OECD Investment Policy Review: China 2018*. OECD Publishing, 2018.

Organisation for Economic Co-Operation and Development. *OECD Science, Technology and Innovation Outlook 2018: Adapting to Technological and Societal Disruption*. OECD Publishing, 2019a.

Organisation for Economic Co-Operation and Development. *OECD Economic Surveys: Ukraine*. OECD Publishing, 2019b.

Organisation for Economic Co-Operation and Development. *Strengthening FDI and SME Linkages in Czechia*. OECD Publishing, May 2024. https:// www.oecd.org/content/dam/oecd/en/publications/reports/2024/05 /strengthening-fdi-and-sme-linkages-in-czechia_2883e1db/4c97d104-en .pdf.

Ospyschev, V., T. Antonenko, and D. Prunenko. "Factors Influencing Foreign Investments." *Ekonomika Ukrainy*, no. 4 (2005): 35–40.

Rajan, Raghuram. " 'Friend-Shoring' Isn't Friendly." Hoover Institution, 2022. https://www.hoover.org/research/friend-shoring-isnt-friendly.

Robinson, Joan. *The Accumulation of Capital*. Macmillan, 1956.

Romer, Paul M. "Endogenous Technological Change." *Journal of Political Economy* 98, no. 5, Part 2 (October 1990): S71–S102. https://doi. org/10.1086/261725.

Solow, Robert M. "A Contribution to the Theory of Economic Growth." *Quarterly Journal of Economics* 70, no. 1 (1956): 65–94. https://doi.org/10.2307 /1884513.

Stanford Center on China's Economy and Institutions. "Friendshoring? Nearshoring? Reshoring? How the U.S. Trade Relationship with China Is Evolving." Stanford University, 2022. https://sccei.fsi.stanford.edu/china-briefs /friendshoring-nearshoring-reshoring-how-us-trade-relationship-china -evolving.

State Council of the People's Republic of China. "Made in China 2025." 2015. http://www.gov.cn/zhengce/content/2015-05/19/content_9784.htm.

State Council of the People's Republic of China. "Notice of the State Council on the Publication of 'Made in China 2025.' " May 8, 2015. Translated by the Center for Security and Emerging Technology. https://cset.georgetown.edu/publication /notice-of-the-state-council-on-the-publication-of-made-in-china-2025/.

Ukraine President. "Strategy of Economic and Social Development of Ukraine 'Through European Integration' for 2004–2015." Decree of the President of Ukraine, April 28, 2004.

United Nations Conference on Trade and Development. "World Investment Report 2003: FDI Policies for Development—National and International Perspectives." United Nations, 2003.

United Nations Conference on Trade and Development. "World Investment Report 2005: Transnational Corporations and the Internationalization of R&D." United Nations, 2005.

United Nations Conference on Trade and Development. "World Investment Report 2020: International Production Beyond the Pandemic." United Nations, 2020.

United Nations Conference on Trade and Development. "3.3 Foreign Direct Investment." *UNCTAD Handbook of Statistics 2023*. https://unctad.org /system/files/official-document/tdstat48_FS09_en.pdf.

United Nations Conference on Trade and Development. "World Investment Report 2023: Investing in Sustainable Energy for All." United Nations, 2023. https://unctad.org/publication/world-investment-report-2023.

United Nations Conference on Trade and Development. "World Investment Report 2024: Investment Facilitation and Digital Government." United Nations, 2024. https://unctad.org/publication/world-investment-report-2024.

United Nations Conference on Trade and Development. "Handbook of Statistics 2024." United Nations, 2025. https://unctad.org/system/files /official-document/tdstat49_en.pdf.

United Nations Conference on Trade and Development. "Foreign Direct Investment: Inward and Outward Flows and Stock, Annual." UNCTADstat Data Centre. Accessed April 7, 2025. https://unctadstat.unctad.org /datacentre/dataviewer/US.FdiFlowsStock.

United Nations Conference on Trade and Development. "World Investment Report 2024: Poland Fact Sheet." Accessed April 7, 2025. https://unctad.org /system/files/non-official-document/wir_fs_pl_en.pdf.

United Nations Conference on Trade and Development. "World Investment Report." United Nations, various years.

U.S. Department of Commerce. "Strategic Plan: FY 2022–2026." 2022.

U.S. Department of Commerce. "Investment Climate Statements: Ukraine." U.S. Department of Commerce, 2023.

U.S. Department of Commerce—National Security Strategy Document U.S. Department of Commerce. "The Decisive Decade: Advancing National Security at the Department of Commerce." 2022.

Welfens, Paul J. J., and Piotr Jasinski. *Privatization and Foreign Direct Investment in Transforming Economies*. Dartmouth Publishing, 1994.

White House. "Bipartisan Infrastructure Law Guidebook." 2022a.

White House. "CHIPS and Science Act of 2022." 2022b.

White House. "Inflation Reduction Act Guidebook." 2022c.

White House. "Remarks by Brian Deese on the Modern American Industrial Strategy." October 13, 2022.

White House. "Remarks by National Security Advisor Jake Sullivan on Renewing American Economic Leadership." April 27, 2023.

World Bank. "Doing Business Reports." World Bank Group, 2005–2015.

World Bank. "Global Investment Competitiveness Report 2019/2020: Rebuilding Investor Confidence in Times of Uncertainty." World Bank, 2020.

World Bank. "China Economic Update: Investing in Growth." World Bank Group, 2023a.

World Bank. "Doing Business 2023." World Bank, 2023b.

World Bank. "Foreign Direct Investment, Net Inflows (% of GDP)." Accessed April 7, 2025. https://data.worldbank.org/indicator/BX.KLT.DINV.WD.GD.ZS.

World Bank. "China Economic Update." World Bank Group, various years.

World Bank, Government of Ukraine, European Union, and United Nations. "Ukraine Rapid Damage and Needs Assessment: February 2022–February 2023." March 2023. https://documents1.worldbank.org/curated/en/099184503212328877/pdf/P1801740d1177f03c0ab180057556615497.pdf.

World Bank Group. "State of Investment Promotion Agencies: Evidence from WAIPA–WBG's Joint Global Survey." World Bank, 2020. https://documents1.worldbank.org/curated/en/499971594008431029/pdf/State-of-Investment-Promotion-Agencies-Evidence-from-WAIPA-WBG-s-Joint-Global-Survey.pdf.

World Economic Forum. "The Global Competitiveness Report 2020: How Countries Are Performing on the Road to Recovery." WEF, 2020.

World Economic Forum. "The Global Competitiveness Report 2024." WEF, 2024.

Yin, Hejun. "China's R&D Expenditure Exceeds 3.3 Trillion Yuan in 2023: Minister." The State Council of the People's Republic of China, March 5, 2024. https://english.www.gov.cn/news/202403/05/content_WS65e6ff4dc6d0868f4e8e4b66.html.

Author Biography

Olga Kugatkina is a business founder, strategist, and board advisor. She advised entrepreneurs and boards on scaling businesses and expanding operations.

With a career spanning Silicon Valley and London, she has led over 200 due diligence assessments and valuations, contributing to the successful execution of more than 114 deals ranging from $100 million to $1 billion. Olga has guided companies through successful exits on the London Stock Exchange, the NYSE, and via strategic sales.

Her expertise extends to providing strategic advice to the U.S. Department of Commerce on cross-border investments and conducting research for the UK Department for Business and Trade. She holds a PhD in International Economics and is an alumna of the Thunderbird School of Global Management at Arizona State University and the Strategic Leadership Program at Stanford University Graduate School of Business.

Index

Printed and bound by CPI Group (UK) Ltd, Croydon, CR0 4YY

16/06/2025

14690052-0001